THE FIRST TE

THE FIRST TEXANS

By

Carolyn Mitchell Burnett

Illustrated by

J. Kay Wilson

EAKIN PRESS ★ Austin, Texas

FIRST EDITION

Copyright © 1995
By Carolyn Mitchell Burnett

Published in the United States of America
By Eakin Press
A Division of Sunbelt Media, Inc.

ISBN 0-89015-980-7

10 9 8 7 6 5 4 3 2

Library of Congress Cataloging-in-Publication Data
Burnett, Carolyn Mitchell.
  The first Texans / Carolyn Mitchell Burnett.
    p.   cm.
  ISBN 0-89015-980-7 : $14.95
  1. Indians of North America — Texas — History — Juvenile literature.
  2. Indians of North America — Texas — Social life and customs — Juvenile literature. [1. Indians of North America — Texas.]
    I. Title
E78.T4B87   1995
976.4'00497 — dc20   94-16986
                                                              CIP
                                                              AC

*I dedicate this book to my husband, Jim.
Without his patience and encouragement
it could never have been written.*

Contents

Introduction

Man first came to the continent of North America, and the place we now call Texas, thousands of years ago. It is believed these early inhabitants crossed the Bering Strait from Siberia into Alaska. They may have crossed the narrow strait in a boat during the summer or glided over ice in the winter. Some may have walked across a dry land bridge that existed several times during the Ice Age. During these times, much of the earth's water was frozen into great sheets of ice that covered the continents. This freezing caused the level of the oceans to be much lower than they are today.

Most of these early people were hunters. It is likely they crossed the Bering Strait into Alaska following game, such as seals, walruses and polar bears, or in search of new game. They began moving slowly southward, settling in all parts of North and South America.

These early people were intelligent and courageous, as well as being very resourceful. Theirs was a continuing battle to find food and shelter for themselves and their families.

Scientists, called archaeologists, have uncovered the remains of prehistoric cultures in different parts of Texas. These artifacts show that people lived here over 15,000 years ago.

One of the oldest sites was found in Denton County, located in North Texas. Workers uncovered an ancient campsite, where fourteen crude stone hearths, or fireplaces, were found. Near the hearths, the bones of animals were also discovered. Some of these animals no longer live on our earth today.

The oldest remains of a person who had once lived in Texas were found on a ranch near Midland, Texas. Bone fragments of a woman who lived over 8,000 years ago were discovered in a shallow hole in the earth. The archaeologists named this ancient woman "Midland Minnie."

We have also learned about these early people from drawings and paintings they left behind. Some of these early writings were called pictographs, and they were usually left on rock walls or animal skins. Most of these pictographs can be found in the western part of Texas, where there is little rainfall. The dry climate has helped preserve the pictographs.

Another kind of drawing left by these ancient people was called petroglyphs. These drawings were carved into the rock. Through the use of symbols and pictures left in the rock we are able to learn more about the customs and religious beliefs of these people who were later called Indians. Also, some Indian maps have been discovered. They too, have been carved into the rocks.

We have also learned about the early Indians through folklore. Folklore consists of songs, stories, and sayings that were told by word of mouth and passed from one generation to another. These included stories of their religious and superstitious beliefs, as well as stories about their every day life.

Some Indians developed very complex societies. The Aztec Indians of Mexico reached a very high cultural level. They understood mathematics and astronomy, and they planned and built beautiful cities. Even though they were not living in Texas, the impact of their culture was felt by the Indians who lived north of the Rio Grande.

The life of the early Indians varied greatly. Each tribe had its own way of life, and whether they became farmers, hunters, or fishermen depended on their environment.

A study of the early Indian culture in our state gives us a better understanding of how the first Texans lived. It also emphasizes the importance of leaving an accurate account of our own history to be studied and enjoyed by those generations who come after us.

MIDLAND MINNIE

I wonder about the woman called Midland Minnie,
Who lived in our land long ago,
I wonder if Minnie were living today,
Would she be a friend, or a foe?

I wonder what kind of woman she was,
Was she happy, or was she sad,
Did she smile when the sun broke through the dark clouds,
Did the stars in the sky make her glad?

I wonder if she worked hard from morning 'til night,
With never much time for play,
Did her mother teach her to cook and to sew,
Did her Grandmother teach her to pray?

I wonder, when death came to take her away,
Flooding her loved ones with grief,
Was she still a young maiden, innocent and pure,
Or, perhaps was she wed to a chief?

My questions will never be answered, that's true,
For there's no written records to show,
What happened to Minnie and all of her kin,
Many thousands of years ago.
      But . . . Still, I wonder!

                           — CAROLYN M. BURNETT

The Coahuiltecans

The Coahuiltecan (ko-ah-WEEL-tay-can) Indians, who are now extinct, lived inland from Galveston Bay to the Rio Grande. Some lived as far west as present day San Antonio. These Indians lived in groups called bands. Each band had its own chief, who was usually chosen because he had been successful in battle, or because he was a good hunter. However, being courageous and brave was not enough. If the chief angered the tribe, a new leader was chosen.

Most band members lived together in harmony, but occasionally an argument would occur. When this happened, the argument was settled in the form of a fistfight. Weapons were never used in a fight within the band. The Indians would fight until one or both of them could go on no longer. When the fight was over, the fighters would sometimes leave the tribe for awhile. Later, when their tempers had cooled, one or both would return to the band and become friends again.

Duties were usually evenly divided between the men and women. However, the Spanish explorer, Cabeza de Vaca, felt women had the hardest job. He noted that out of a 24-hour period a woman could only rest for six hours. She was busy baking, hauling wood and water, caring for the children, and doing other household chores.

Each Coahuiltecan band claimed a certain area of

1

land, and anyone who trespassed on that land was attacked. Since these Indians were nomads they returned to the same places year after year to claim their land. They usually only stayed in one place a few days.

The Coahuiltecans had very few natural resources. Their land was a dry, rolling plain, covered with mesquite, prickly pear, and brush. They lived a hard and difficult life.

FOOD

Because of their harsh enviornment, the Coahuiltecans had to use any food that was available to them. Some bands in the river valleys were able to gather pecans. Others harvested large quantities of beans from mesquite thickets. The sweet, nutritious mesquite beans grew in pods that measured from four to seven inches long. When the mesquite beans were plentiful, the Indians dried them. The dried beans were then pounded into coarse flour to be stored for future use.

Those bands living near large streams killed fish, using their bow and arrow. At night they used lighted torches to attract the fish, and in shallow streams they used large fishing nets called seines. Sometimes the fish were not cleaned, but were roasted and set aside for seven to eight days. When flies and insects had covered the fish, it was believed they were ready to eat. This was thought to be a special treat to be enjoyed by every member of the band.

All available plants were used by the Coahuiltecans. The agave plant supplied one of their main foods. The bulbs were roasted in pits, ground into flour, and then eaten. During the winter, a drink called mescal was made from the leaves of the agave plant. The prickly pear produced a fruit that became one of their favorite foods. They even dried the skin of the pear and ground it into flour. The juice of the prickly pear was squeezed into a pit that was dug in the ground. Then, they dipped the juice out of the pit and drank it. They stored their water and food in gourds that had been hollowed out.

Since these Indians had no horses, they hunted animals entirely on foot. It is said that a Coahuiltecan hunter could run after a deer all day long and still not be tired. Sometimes the hunters would hide sharp stakes behind barriers set up along the trail. When the deer tried to jump the barrier, it fell on the stake and was killed. Wild pigs, called javelinas, were caught in cleverly concealed pits. These pits were dug so the trapped animal could not move about, making it easier for the hunter to kill the animal quickly.

Sometimes the hunters used the "surround" method to capture their game. A "surround" was when a large group of hunters formed a circle around the animals. As the hunters moved toward the center of the circle, the animals became trapped inside. This made it easier for the kill. Occasionally, brush fires were used to stampede the animals.

The Coahuiltecans did not overlook any source of food. They ate spiders, ant eggs, worms, lizards, and snakes. At times they were even known to eat rotten wood and dirt. When food was found, the Coahuiltecans tried to store some for later use. They hollowed out prickly pear leaves for the containers. Mesquite flour and water were stored in gourds. Some of the bands wove baskets and made net from fiber. They used a large net tied to sticks to carry their heavy loads.

CLOTHING

The Coahuiltecans wore very little clothing. The men usually wore a breechcloth that reached below their knees. The breechcloth was brightly decorated with seeds, animal teeth, and any other ornaments they could find. Necklaces made of bones, shells, and feathers were

also worn. In cold weather, they wore robes of rabbit or coyote skins. The skins were cut, twisted into strands like a rope, and sewn together. They also used animal skins for blankets and cloaks.

The women wore short buckskin skirts. Both men and women went barefoot or wore sandals made of fiber. They also tattooed their bodies to distinguish one band from another.

SHELTER

The Coahuiltecans had small moveable shelters for their homes. They placed reed mats and animal hides over bent willow saplings. These formed a dome-shaped hut.

Fires for cooking and heating were built inside each hut, and even though the sides of the huts were open, a lot of smoke still stayed inside the dwelling.

These huts were built in a thicket, and trenches were dug around the camp. From these trenches the Indians could shoot their arrows at anyone who might be attacking them.

Their brush lean-to dwellings were suitable to the nomadic life of the Coahuiltecans. Since their only means of travel was walking, they had to carry all their belongings on their backs. The mats and hides could be quickly rolled up, placed on their backs, and moved to the next camp.

WEAPONS AND TOOLS

The main weapon of the Coahuiltecans was the bow and arrow. The bow was usually made from a strong mesquite root, and the string of the bow came from deer sinew. Their long arrows were tipped with flint and decorated with feathers.

Another useful weapon used by the Coahuiltecans was a curved wooden club called a "rabbit stick." It was thrown like a boomerang at rabbits and other small brush animals. They also used the "rabbit stick" for digging, scraping, and prying.

Other crude tools, such as hammers, scrapers, axes, and knives were made from flint and used by the Coahuiltecans.

CUSTOMS AND RELIGION

If a Coahuiltecan band chose to challenge another band to war, it was the custom for one of the warriors to go to the enemy camp. The warrior would shoot his arrows into a tree and perform a war dance. This challenged his enemies to war. The enemy usually responded in the same manner, and the warrior returned to camp to report the outcome of his challenge.

After a war, if there was a victory, the warriors returned to the band to perform the scalp dance. These warriors always stopped just before reaching camp so all the band members could rush out to meet them. Then, they placed the enemy scalps they had taken on poles and placed the poles in a line. First the warriors danced around the poles. Then the women, who had smeared their faces with charcoal, danced around the poles.

When a warrior was killed, his wife would tear the hair from the crown of her head. She would then cut the rest of her hair short, roll around in the dust, and slash herself several times with a flint knife.

Men would also slash themselves with stones if some of their relatives had died. However, the men did not tear out their hair. Close relatives, like a son or brother, were mourned for three months. During this time, those in mourning would never leave their huts. Friends and relatives brought food to them during this mourning period.

The Coahuiltecans believed in spirits, demons, and

other supernatural beings. Their religious ceremonies were overseen by the "shaman," who also served as their medicine man. The shaman was believed to have the power to cure those who were ill.

Their religious ceremonies consisted of dances and festivals, called mitotes. The mitotes would begin late in the evening when friends and relatives from adjoining bands would begin to arrive.

A large fire was built for cooking the food. Then, the music and dancing would begin. Music was provided by rattles made from dried gourds, and a drum made by stretching coyote hide over a wooden hoop. The dancers circled the fire in perfect rhythm to the sound of the drum. They moved around the circle in a series of hops, dancing through the night without stopping. Peyote juice, made from the peyote cactus plant, was passed around the circle from time to time. At daybreak, the guests would leave the camp, taking food and drink with them when they left.

The mitotes were usually held during the summer months when food was more plentiful, as it was a time of thanksgiving. They also had a mitote to celebrate a victory in war.

The Coahuiltecans looked forward to their special ceremonies and celebrations. It was a time when they could visit with friends and relatives. It was also a time for the bands to exchange food and other items with each other. Even though it lasted a short time, the mitote was the highlight of the year for these Indian bands.

CHILDREN

Coahuiltecan babies were carried on their mother's back. The child's arms were placed around the mother's neck, and his body was tied around her with animal skins.

At a very early age, children were given small bows and arrows. These were not toys, but were used as weapons for hunting their own food supply. Boys were taken on hunting trips and war parties. They became lookouts for the warriors and performed small chores for the hunters.

When it was time for the children to pass from childhood into adulthood, the shaman held a ceremony and the children were tattooed. To do this, long shallow cuts were made in their skin. Charcoal and resin were then rubbed into the open wound. The children did not cry out no matter how painful it was for them. Boys were considered ready for manhood only after they had proven themselves to be good hunters.

CONCLUSION

There are very few areas on the North American continent more difficult for people to live on than the land of the Coahuiltecans. It was necessary for them to use everything they had for their existence. They had to know which plants could be eaten and which were poisonous. They had to remember when fruits would be ripe in certain areas and when game could be found. However, the Coahuiltecans seemed content with their harsh environment.

Many of the Coahuiltecans traveled to Mexico and joined bands there. Later, explorers from Europe came, bringing with them epidemics of measles and smallpox. By 1800, the bands of Coahuiltecan Indians had gradually become extinct.

THE KARANKAWAS

The Karankawa (kah-RANK-eh-wah) Indians lived in the region that extended from Galveston Island to Corpus Christi Bay along the Gulf of Mexico. This flat prairie land contained several marshy areas and a few wooded regions on the gulf. The land of the Karankawa Indians did not extend further than one hundred miles inland.

The Karankawas were first seen by the survivors of the Narvaez Expedition in 1528. When Cabeza de Vaca and his companions tried to leave, their shipwrecked boat began to fill with water and three men were drowned. The others were left half-naked and dying from the cold. The Karankawa Indians rescued the men and took them to their huts, where they built a fire.

However, the Spanish explorers were never able to establish a good relationship with the Karankawas. Some of the Indians did go to the missions that were established by the Spanish, but most of them wanted nothing to do with the mission system of life.

The Karankawas lived in small bands of thirty or forty people. The bands were composed of relatives, and each band had its own chief . When the food and water supply became scarce, the bands were subdivided into smaller groups, giving them a better chance for survival.

The chores of the camp were given to the women.

Their jobs included putting up the hut, gathering wood for the cooking, and taking down the hut when the band was ready to move on. The men hunted larger game and fished.

The name Karankawa meant "dog lovers." The dog was very important to the Karankawas, and every band had several. The dog was more than a pet to them. They used them to hunt wild game, as well as for guarding their camps.

The Karankawas were a nomadic group of Indians, seldom spending more than a few weeks at each camp. It was necessary for them to move often in order to find enough food to survive. They would return year after year to places where they had once found food.

FOOD

The Karankawa Indians met their need for food by hunting animals and gathering plants they found around their camps. They hunted small game such as javelinas and deer. Bison, bear, and other large animals were hunted only if they came near the coastal area. The Karankawa would not travel outside their territory to hunt these larger animals. They also gathered berries, nuts, seeds, and other plant foods they found along the shore.

They cooked the foods they found in clay pots, which were placed on live coals of the fires they had built. The men would coat the inside of the pots with tar to make them waterproof.

Their largest food supply came from the water. In the fall, they lived on islands in the Gulf of Mexico, where they were able to harvest roots of underwater plants. They also caught clams, oysters, turtles, alligators, and scallops. When winter came, they returned to the mainland, where they were supplied with oysters they found along the shore. In spring and summer they supplemented their diet of berries, fruits, and game with fish.

Dugout canoes were used for fishing. These were made from the trunks of trees with the bark left on. One side of the log was trimmed flat. Then, by burning and scraping, the center of the log was hollowed out. The canoe was made large enough to hold a man, his wife, children, and all of his possessions. Poles, rather than paddles, were used to move the canoes along. These long poles were pushed against the bottom of a shallow stream close to the shore.

They had no fish hooks for fishing, so they used their bow and arrows instead. Some fish were also caught in traps they had set.

Since most of their food supply came from the water, the Karankawas needed to protect themselves against mosquitos. To do this, they used a generous supply of alligator grease. The alligator fat was melted, and then smeared over their entire body. The grease had a strong odor, and was very helpful in keeping the mosquitos away.

Oysters were another food enjoyed by the Karankawa Indians. They brought their catch of oysters and threw them into the fire. When the heat of the fire caused the shells to open, they were raked out and eaten.

Seeds and nuts were gathered when they were available. They were crushed by stones and used in stews or made into dough and baked in the ashes. When corn meal was available, they made it into cakes to be baked in hot coals.

When food became scarce for the Karankawas, they were forced to eat locusts, bear fat, and tallow. They would eat raw meat, and like the Coahuiltecans they enjoyed eating food that had been allowed to spoil. It was necessary for the Karankawa Indians to make use of any food that was available to them.

CLOTHING

The Karankawa Indians were tall, strong, and well-built. The average male was over six feet tall, and the average female was five feet, five inches tall. They were the tallest of the Texas tribes.

The men wore little or no clothing during the summer months. They liked to brag of how strong they were, and they would stay in the burning hot sun without clothes, always avoiding the shade. Then when winter came and the water in the rivers was solid ice, they would go out in the early morning, break the ice with their bodies, and take a bath. Sometimes during the winter months they would wear robes of fur, but they always went barefoot no matter what the temperature might be.

The Karankawa Indians decorated their faces and bodies with tattoos. They wore bracelets, anklets, necklaces, and put feathers in their hair. They also adorned their bodies with pieces of cane. The cane was pushed through holes they made in their lower lip, and on each side of their chest.

When they were on the warpath, they would paint half their face black, and the other half red. A breechcloth, or apron, with a long sash was also worn. The sash was trimmed with fringe and tassels, which almost touched the ground in the back.

The women usually wore skirts made of deerskin. However, they sometimes made them of Spanish moss, which they tied at the waist with a piece of rawhide. They wore shawls of Spanish moss, which they draped over their left shoulder.

The women who were married would paint themselves with stripes. Sometimes they would add other figures, such as birds, flowers, or animals to the stripes. The unmarried women had only a small stripe on their foreheads which would come to a point at their nose. It would then go through the middle of their lips, and as far down as their chins.

SHELTER

Because the Karankawa Indians were nomads, their homes had to be easily dismantled and put back together again. Their huts were made of a dozen or more slender willow poles. These poles were about eighteen feet long and were pointed at one end. They were tied with a strip of rawhide to form an oval framework. Skins and woven mats were then thrown over the frame. Usually, only one side was covered for a windbreak.

The size of the hut varied, but they were usually made ten or twelve feet in diameter. This made the hut large enough for seven or eight people.

The Karankawas built fires for cooking and heating in the center of the hut. Since most of the hut was open, the smoke was never trapped inside.

They placed animal skins inside the huts. These could be used to sit on, or they could wrap themselves in the skins when it was very cold, or when they were sleeping. There were no other furnishings inside the hut.

Whenever it was possible, they built their huts near a stream. This made it easier for them to obtain food and water.

When it was time for the Karankawas to move on, they removed the skins from the poles and placed them in the canoe. They often left the poles behind so they would be ready for use when they returned.

WEAPONS AND TOOLS

One of the most important weapons of the Karankawa Indians was the bow and arrow. The bow was made from cedar and was as long as the man was tall. They made their bowstrings of deer sinew, or tendon. Several pieces of fine sinew were twisted together to make the strings stronger. Then they would attach three feathers to each of their arrows.

Other weapons used by the Karankawas were lances, clubs, and a small axe called a tomahawk. They used the tomahawk for a tool and a weapon as well. It was used for chopping wood, driving sticks into the ground, and killing animals.

CUSTOMS AND RELIGION

Small family groups, or bands, were brought together by the use of smoke signals. These smoke signals were used for social events or war. Each band had its own chief, even though he did not have much power. The chief was usually the oldest member of the band.

Marriage in the bands was arranged by the parents. When a marriage had been arranged, the man brought gifts to the girl's family.

A man was not allowed to go inside the hut of his in-laws. They were never to speak to each other, and if they should happen to meet face-to-face, they would both turn their heads to avoid looking at each other.

The Karankawas practiced a great deal of ceremony and ritual when a death occurred in the band. This was especially true if the death was that of a boy or young man, who would be mourned for an entire year. Before dawn, at noon, and at sunset, the parents and all the relatives would weep for the boy that had died. When the year was over, a ceremony was performed that would make all the mourners pure.

Like the Coahuiltecans, when a son or brother died, the family did not provide themselves with food for three months. Their friends and relatives would bring food to them in their huts. Only those that were very old were not mourned. They believed the old were a burden to others, were not happy, and therefore they were better off dead.

The dead were buried in shallow graves, usually

near a campsite. The shaman, or medicine man, was not buried. He was cremated during a very special ceremony. One year later, the shaman's ashes were mixed with water and then drunk by all his relatives. The Karankawas believed that by drinking the ashes, they would receive the powers of the shaman for themselves.

Their religious practices were centered around ceremonies called "mitotes." One mitote was considered to be of great religious importance and was celebrated after successful hunting and fishing trips. It became a form of thanksgiving for them. They built a fire inside an enlarged hut, and on the fire they would make a yellow tea from the leaves of a shrub called yaupon. From the moment it was removed from the fire, the men would begin to chant, "Who Wishes To Drink?" When the women heard this cry, they would stop whatever they were doing and remain motionless. If a woman moved, she was in danger of being punished. If a woman passed by while the tea was boiling, the tea had to be thrown away. They believed that if the drink was contaminated by a woman, the men who drank the tea would become sick and die.

Whether or not a mitote ceremony was happy or sad was determined by the sounds of the music. For the happy mitotes, a tambourine made from a tortoise shell, or a half gourd, was played. For the sad mitotes, harsh, sad cries were made by the Indians. These were done with gestures as they jumped and leaped in a circle. For this mitote they would light a large fire and dance around it without stopping. These might last as long as three days and three nights. The Indian women never took part in these dances. They stood at a distance, with their hair hanging over their faces, shouting sadly.

Other than the ceremonial mitote, the Karankawas had very little social life. Men and boys would shoot arrows at targets, or throw knives and other weapons at a target. They also played some kind of ball and held wrestling matches for entertainment.

There have been some accounts of cannibalism practiced by both the Karankawas and the Coahuiltecans. This custom was not due to hunger, but for the magical powers they believed they could acquire. They believed in this way they would be able to gain the strength and power of their enemies.

CHILDREN

The Karankawas were very fond of their children and treated them with love and kindness. The children were nursed until they were twelve years old. It was a necessity, because many times the Karankawas went several days without food, and the children were allowed to nurse in order to survive.

All of the children were given two names. One was a nickname and was used only by outsiders. The other name was a secret name, and it was thought to have a magical meaning of some kind.

Babies spent most of their time fastened to a cradleboard. This thin board was covered with moss and cloth. It caused the baby's head to slope and tended to flatten the heads of the babies.

As soon as they were physically able, the girls helped their mothers with the work in the camp. At a very early age, the young boys went with their fathers and learned to hunt and fish.

Since survival was hard for these Indians, the children did not lead a carefree life. They had to hunt for their own food at an early age.

As they grew older, ceremonies were held to transform them from childhood into adulthood. The shaman conducted these ceremonies, and part of the ceremony included tattooing each of the children.

CABEZA DE VACA AND THE KARANKAWA

A Spanish explorer named Cabeza de Vaca (kah-BAY-zah day VAH-kah) was one of the first explorers in Texas. He came with an expedition led by Panfilo de Narvaez (nar-VAH-ez) in 1528. Their plan was to explore Florida and look for gold. They did not find any gold, and when they returned to the coast for their ships they were not there.

The explorers built crude boats with the hope of sailing to Mexico. However, about five weeks after they had set sail they were hit by a hurricane. Most of the boats were wrecked and many of the explorers drowned.

One of the ships that survived the storm was commanded by Cabeza de Vaca. He and his men landed on an island believed to be Galveston Island. The explorers later called the island "The Isle of Misfortune."

The Karankawa Indians discovered the poor Spanish explorers and felt sorry for them. They brought the men food and cared for their needs. They were friendly to the Spanish explorers.

After a few days rest, the men decided to continue their journey. However, when they put their boat into the water, a huge wave hit the boat turning it over. Several of the men were drowned and the rest came back to shore. They were naked and freezing. Again, the Karankawa Indians came to help the Spanish explorers. They took them to their village, built warm fires and gave them food. If it had not been for the Karankawas, Cabeza de Vaca and his men would have surely died.

The winter was very hard on the explorers and Indians as well. It was extremely cold for that part of Texas and food supplies soon ran dangerously low. Also, many of the Indians and explorers became ill and several of them died. The Spanish had no choice. They had to become part of the Indian society if they were to survive. They hunted for berries and other foods. They

17

fished alongside the Indians. But, the explorers wanted to leave the Indian way of life and make their way to Mexico where many of their countrymen were. However, the Indians did not want them to leave because the Spanish had become very helpful to them.

Finally, after six years with the Karankawa Indians, Cabeza de Vaca and three other explorers were able to escape and make their way to Mexico.

CONCLUSION

The Karankawa Indians were constantly faced with the problems of finding enough food and water to stay alive. They found it difficult to have even a meager existence in their nomadic way of life. Yet, they seemed happy.

It is difficult for us to understand how the Karankawas could prefer their own gods, food, and customs, rather than accept the opportunities offered by the Europeans. But, they favored their own lifestyle and did not want to change.

The white man brought to the Karankawas diseases which they were unable to overcome. Because of this, their population decreased, and they eventually became an extinct tribe. It is believed that after 1858, there were no Karankawa Indians left in Texas. Some survivors of these Indians may have been absorbed into the population of Mexico.

THE JUMANOS

The Jumano (hoo-MAH-no) Indians lived along the Rio Grande, the driest part of Texas. The Jumanos were thought to be descendents of the pit dwellers who lived in Texas between 2,000 to 5,000 years ago. They lived in an area that stretched from Big Bend to El Paso, where the Rio Grande winds its way through tall mountains and dusty plateaus. Due to lack of rain in this area, large sections of their land were considered to be desert land.

Archaeologists believe the Jumano Indians were members of a Pueblo civilization from the Southwest. The villages of the Pueblo Indians were scattered through the states of Arizona, New Mexico, and Utah, and so it would be quite natural for them to extend to Texas as well.

In 1535, Cabeza de Vaca and his companions came to the land of the Jumano Indians. They found the Jumanos different from any of the other tribes they had seen in Texas. Other tribes of Indians had come out to meet these Spanish explorers, but the Jumanos stayed in their houses. However, this did not mean the Spanish were not welcome. The Jumanos had already prepared special houses for them and presented the explorers with presents of skin blankets. When the explorers went into these houses, they found the Indians seated with their faces turned toward the wall. They each had their heads down with their hair pulled over their eyes. They had placed their property in a heap in the center of the floor. It is thought the Jumanos believed these Spanish explorers were some kind of white "gods."

Cabeza de Vaca compared these Indians to the Karankawas in size and method of dress. The Spanish noted that the Jumanos had at least one chief of each village. Some villages had two chiefs, a chief of war, and a chief of peace. Although there were differences among the various villages, they were friendly toward each other.

Of all the Indians in Texas, less is known about the Jumanos than any other tribe. It is believed when years of drought began to occur more frequently, the settlements began to falter. Even though some stayed with the land, trying to raise enough food to stay alive, many of the Jumano Indians moved on to places where more water could be found. Some of them became bison hunters on the southern plains.

Eventually, the Jumano, like the Coahuiltecans and Karankawas, simply vanished from Texas. Diseases, such as smallpox, whooping cough, and measles killed many of these Indians. Some who survived are believed to have gone to Mexico and became a part of the Mexican society. Much of what we know about the Jumano Indians comes from artifacts and pictographs they left behind.

FOOD

The Jumano Indians were mostly farmers. Since they lived in such a dry area of Texas, they tried to make good use of water from the Rio Grande. They planted their crops as close to the river as possible. When they had enough water, they were able to grow corn, squash, pumpkins, and other vegetables. It is not certain if both men and women worked in the fields. However, it is likely that maintaining the crops was the men's job, following the custom of the Pueblo Indians.

The Jumanos used corn in many different ways. Sometimes they would boil or roast the ears whole. Other times they would remove the kernels from the cob and cook them. They also ground the kernels into flour so they could be made in to corn cakes, which were baked in hot ashes. For a special treat, they added berries or dried meat to the corn cakes before baking.

When they were unable to grow crops during very dry years, it was necessary for the Jumanos to find wild foods. One of the most important wild foods was the mesquite bean. These beans were very difficult to remove from the pods. Since the pods were also edible, some of the Indians ate the pod and all. The pods were also ground into a coarse flour to be stored and used whenever it was needed. We still use mesquite beans today, though not for human consumption. They are used for horse feed.

The Jumanos also used the bulbs of the agave plant. They cooked them in earth ovens. They also ate prickly pear and the fruits of other cactus plants.

The Jumanos prepared their food by a method known as stone boiling. To stone boil their food, they heated stones in a fire. When the stones were hot enough, they used tongs made of sticks to pick them up and drop them into a container that was partly filled with water. When the water started to boil, the food to be cooked was added. As the stones cooled, they were thrown out and replaced by more hot ones.

The Jumanos also had pottery, but seemed to prefer the stone boiling method of preparing their food. They also used gourds for containers. Sometimes they prepared a piece of rawhide, pressed it into a hole they had dug in the ground, and used it as a container.

When food was scarce, some of the Indian men hunted buffalo. They traveled through the Davis Mountains to the northern plains. Until the Spanish came, the Indians had no horses and had to walk these long distances. This made it difficult to get the buffalo back to the village. They either carried the hides and meat on their backs or hauled them on a dog travois. The travois was made by stretching a piece of hide between two long poles. The buffalo meat and skins were placed on the stretched piece of hide, and the two long poles were attached to the dog for pulling. Because the Indians were walking, and it was a long journey home, they prepared the meat before leaving the hunting area. They dried the meat and cut it into long strips of jerky. This kept it from spoiling before they returned to the village.

CLOTHING

The Spanish explorers noted that the Jumanos were very clean and neat. They used the skin of the buffalo to cover their bodies. The women wore deerskin tops similar to the ponchos we wear today. They also used deerskin to make skirts, and carried cloaks made from tanned skins of their cattle.

The men wore little or no clothing, usually only a long breechcloth. This was made from two strips of tanned hide and held together by a narrow strip of hide.

The Jumanos wore their hair long and tied close to their head. The men cut their hair very short up to the middle of their heads. It was then left two fingers long and curled with paint so it had the appearance of a cap on their heads. On the crown of the head they left a large lock of hair where they fastened goose, crane, and hawk feathers. The women wore their hair loose and tied close to their heads like the men.

Thread was made from twisted cotton and used to tie ornaments around their necks. They also made turquoise and coral bands to be used as nose and ear decorations.

SHELTER

The Jumano Indians lived in homes called pueblos, similar to those of the Pueblo Indians. The pueblo was built with adobe bricks. These bricks were made from a mixture of moist clay, ashes, and sometimes dry grass. After the bricks had been formed, they were left to dry in the sun. The adobe bricks were so strong they could last for hundreds of years.

The houses were built low and square with the lower half built below the ground level. The roofs of the pueblos were flat and very strong. The Jumanos probably used saplings and brush covered with adobe to strengthen them. Their homes were sturdy enough for the Indians to stand on the roofs without damage to the pueblo. Since the homes were built half in and half out of the ground, they were dark and cool during the hot summer months. They also painted the walls yellow, red and black, and arranged their homes around a central plaza.

Later, most of the Jumano Indians became buffalo hunters, replacing their adobe homes with tents made from animal skins.

WEAPONS AND TOOLS

Very little is known about the tools and weapons of the Jumano Indians. It is believed they used long, sharp pointed sticks for digging when they were planting their crops.

The Spanish explorers noted that the Jumanos used the bow and arrow for hunting. The string of the bow was made from sinew. They often carried shields made from the hide of the buffalo.

CUSTOMS AND RELIGION

As noted earlier, the Jumanos had a strange way of greeting their guests. They stayed in their pueblos, but prepared a special house for the visitors. Sometimes they made musical sounds, similar to a flute, with their mouths. They offered their guests gifts, such as buffalo skins, bows and arrows, and a variety of foods.

Many times visitors would be entertained by dances and celebrations. The Indians and their guests would sit around the campfire. They made music by beating their hands together in a rhythmical fashion.

CHILDREN

Very little is known about the Jumano children. It is likely they helped their parents tend the crops. As they grew older, they were probably taught how to hunt, prepare the buffalo skins, and perform other tasks Indian children learned.

CONCLUSION

Of all the Indian tribes in Texas less is known about the Jumano than any other tribe. We do know they were successful for a time in establishing homes along the Rio Grande. Then when the droughts came, their settlements began to fail.

Some Jumanos tried to stay with their sun parched lands and grow whatever foods they could in the hardened soil. Some moved to areas where water was more plentiful, while others became buffalo hunters on the southern plains.

Eventually the Jumano Indians disappeared from Texas.

THE CADDOES

The Caddo (CAD-do) Confederacies, located in the Piney Woods of East Texas were very important to the state of Texas. More than twenty-four confederacies made up the Caddo nation, and each had its own tribal government.

Each Caddo tribe had two chiefs, called the Caddi. One chief settled matters of war and peace, and the other took charge of religious matters for the tribe. The chiefs had many helpers, including both men and women. Many times these helpers would be war heroes.

Some tribes had a woman as one of their chiefs. The Caddo people believed that all people came from a female god and her two daughters. In one particular tribe, a woman chief called "The Great Lady," lived in a house with many rooms and with many servants.

The largest Caddo Confederacy was the Hasinai (HAH-seen-eye) tribe. Members of this tribe called each other Tayshas (TAY-sahs), meaning friends. When the Spanish explorers came, they met a tribe of Caddo Indians called Tejas (TAY-hahs). They thought this was the name of their land. Over the years, "land of the Tejas" was shortened and given the English spelling. Eventually, Tejas became Texas, the name of our state today.

The Caddo Indians lived in what is known as the Piney Woods of Texas, near the Louisiana border. Theirs was a land filled with dense forests, containing a variety of large pine trees. Within these forests were many kinds of wild game, including black bear, deer, and buffalo.

The Caddoes had their first encounter with the Spanish explorers in 1541. Hernando de Soto, who was exploring in Arkansas, sent a party of men to the land that is now Texas.

A Frenchman, Rene Robert Cavelier Sieur de la Salle (lah SAL), was the next explorer into the land of the Caddoes. From Fort St. Louis, located near present-day Victoria, he sent men to find the Mississippi River, and they reached one of the Caddo villages. They continued to explore beyond the village, but La Salle became ill and had to turn back. The Hasinais were so friendly to the explorers, that many of the Frenchmen deserted La Salle and stayed in the village.

FOOD

The Caddoes were very successful farmers and raised an abundance of garden produce. Their most important crop was corn, and they planted two different crops each year. The first crop was called "little corn," and was planted after the rainy season ended. It was ready to harvest in five to six weeks. As soon as the harvest was completed, "flour corn" was planted on the same land. It was ready for harvest in about three months.

The best ears of corn from each harvest were hung in their houses. They placed them where they could be well smoked. Enough seed corn was saved for at least two more years' plantings, in case of drought or crop failures.

The Caddoes also raised beans, squash, sunflower seeds, pumpkins, melons, and tobacco. They had five or six kinds of beans, including pole beans.

The men and women worked together to plant and harvest the crops. The men did the hardest work of clear-

ing the fields and preparing them for planting. Then, the women planted the crops and cared for them during the growing season. The crops were planted in gardens shared by everyone in the tribe. First, the crops of the chief of the village were planted. Crops of the chief's helpers were planted next, and finally crops of the other members of the tribe were planted.

The Caddo men hunted wild game, such as deer, wild hogs, bear, and buffalo for meat. They were very clever hunters and would imitate a deer by disguising themselves with the antlers and hide of the deer.

When horses were introduced to the Caddoes, they began to hunt bear and buffalo. They usually did their hunting in the winter after the crops had all been harvested. Also, during the winter season the bears had become fatter and the buffalo herds were much larger. Buffalo was hunted for the meat, and bears were mostly hunted for their fat. This fat could be preserved and stored in pots for long periods of time.

The Caddoes added many small birds, prairie chickens, ducks, and turkeys to their food supply. These were usually hunted with the help of their dogs.

The Caddo Indians were very good fishermen. They had one interesting method of fishing, called a trotline. They hung short lines, about a foot apart, from a long line. Each line had a hook attached that had been baited with a piece of meat. One end of the line was weighted down with something heavy, and dropped into the stream. The other end was tied to a tree or their boat. The lines were left for a short period of time before they were checked. The fish caught on these hooks were taken off and the lines set once again. Trotline methods of fishing have been handed down through the generations and is still widely used today, thanks to Native Americans.

A variety of nuts were also gathered by the Caddo

Indians. They harvested pecans, chestnuts, acorns, and others. The forests also gave them fruits such as plums, mulberries, grapes, blackberries, and cherries.

Preparation of food for the family was done by the women. Corn was usually roasted by placing the unhusked ears in a bed of ashes. Sometimes the corn was boiled with other vegetables to make a dish called succotash. Large mortars, made from hollowed-out tree trunks, were used for grinding dried corn. The women pounded the corn with large wooden pestles to make flour. The flour was used in soups, breads, and tortillas.

The Caddo Indians had special ways of preserving their food. They put corn, with ashes sprinkled throughout, into large baskets. The ashes were used to keep weevils and other bugs out of the corn. Fish was smoked to keep it from spoiling, and the meat of animals was made into jerky.

CLOTHING

Most of the clothing for the Caddo Indians was made from buckskin, since they were excellent tanners. By using a certain amount of buffalo and deer brains, mixed with the skins, they were able to produce a beautiful black leather.

The women wore sleeveless blouses and skirts made from deerskin. Their skirts were fringed at the hem and trimmed with colorful seeds sewn along the bottom. They wore breechcloths underneath their clothing made of straw and grass. The higher ranking women, probably the wives of the chiefs, wore clothing made of cloth woven from mulberry bark. In winter they wore fur caps made from deer and buffalo skins. They oiled their hair, parted it down the middle, and braided it in one long braid down their backs. It was then tied with rabbit or snake skin that had been dyed red.

When it was warm, the men wore only a breechcloth. As the weather became cooler, they added leggings for warmth. Both men and women wore moccasins.

Hair styles changed from one tribe to another. Usually a man's hair grew about two inches long all over his head, except for a small area on top. The hair in that spot sometimes grew down to his waist, and feathers were attached to it. Shaving off all the hair, except for a narrow band extending over the head from the forehead to the neck was another popular style worn by the men.

The Caddo Indians adorned themselves with bones, seeds, animal teeth, feathers, and shells. They pierced their ears in several places so they could hang ornaments from them. The name Caddo means "pierced nose," and the men of the tribe also pierced their noses and hung ornaments from them.

Tattooing was done on both men and women of the tribe. They used sharp pointed objects to pierce the skin making it bleed. Then they rubbed charcoal into the wounds. When the wounds had healed, the charcoal that remained underneath the skin made tattoos. They made these tattoos from the top of their forehead, through their nose, and to the end of their chin. Plants and animals were their favorite tattooing designs. The women liked tattoos at the corner of their eyes, decorated with streaks of bright colors and designs.

SHELTER

The Caddoes built large, round houses that looked like beehives. These houses had two narrow doorways and no windows. A large hole was left in the top of the house, and smoke from the fire that burned in the center of the house escaped through this opening.

Building a house was a very important activity for the Caddo Indians, and all the people in the village worked together until a house was completed. When a family decided it was time to build a house, they notified the chief. With the help of other officials he decided when the work would begin and who would help with the building.

Those who were selected to bring poles for the house came early in the morning to begin their work. They dug fifteen to twenty holes in a circle and placed a strong pole in each of them. In the center of the circle they erected another pole with a crosspiece attached to the top. Two men climbed the pole, and working together they lassoed the poles in the outer circle and pulled them to the center pole. These poles were tied together with wet leather straps. When this was completed, other workers covered the framework with grapevines, saplings, and other timber. Then another group of workers, usually women, covered the sides with a thick covering of grass and mud. The temporary center pole was cut off at ground level, shelves were built to store food from the harvest, and the house was ready for the Caddo family.

Sometimes two smaller huts were built near the larger house. These were used for working, resting, and storing things.

While the house was being built, the family who would live in it kept busy preparing a feast of roast venison and corn for a house raising bee. The food was first served to the chief, then other officials, and finally the workers. It was always a festive occasion for everyone in the village.

The Caddoes used reeds to make mats for their beds. These mats were placed on forked sticks to raise them off the ground. They were then covered with deerskin or buffalo hide.

WEAPONS AND TOOLS

The Caddoes made crude tools from their available resources. Hoes were usually made from the shoulder blade of a buffalo. They also made digging instruments from strong pieces of wood found in the area.

31

If a piece of land needed to be cleared for planting, they would sometimes burn over the fields rather than dig up the remnants of the old crop. This saved valuable time and energy for the Caddoes and needed no special tools.

With the abundance and variety of trees in the Piney Woods, the Caddoes were able to make strong bows and arrows for use in battle. However, "hit and run" raids seemed to be their most frequent kind of warfare.

CUSTOMS AND RELIGION

The religious practices of the Caddo Indians centered around the temples. The temples looked very much like their houses, except they were larger. In the center of the temple a fire was kept burning at all times, with four large logs pointing to the north, south, east, and west. An altar made of reed mats was placed along one side of the door. Every temple also had benches along the walls and a bed for the temple priest. In front of the bed was a square, wooden bench where the pipe, tobacco, and pottery dishes were kept. These were for used for burnt offerings.

Two small houses were built near the temple for two young boys. The Caddoes believed the great supreme being had sent them to help the Caddoes. Their duty was to listen to the supreme being, tell the priests what they had heard, and the priests would tell the people. No one was allowed to see these boys. The people believed this would cause instant death to them or their families.

Sometimes, when the priest felt the people were not contributing enough food for him and the gods, he would call the elders and tribal leaders to the temple. First, he burned tobacco and buffalo fat as an offering to the gods. Then, to shut out all the outside noises, he closed the door leaving them in total darkness. The leaders listened as the priest changed his voice and began to speak to the young boys, asking them to tell God that the Caddo people were going to be better people and asking that they be given a great harvest, good health, success in battle, and fine hunting. When the priest had finished his prayers, he threw a gourd rattle to the ground. If the rattle did not make any sound, the people were told God was angry with them. The elders and tribal leaders were very frightened when the rattle was silent and made many promises to God.

Each tribe had at least one shaman, or medicine man. Their primary purpose was to cure those who were ill. Tobacco and herbs, used in a variety of ways, was one of their main methods of healing.

The first-fruit rites, which marked the beginning of the harvest, was one of their most important religious ceremonies. The two young men and the priest were honored at this ceremony with a great feast. The people danced and feasted, but the priest went without food or sleep for several days. He was praying and asking God for a good harvest for his people.

The Caddoes had an interesting custom concerning marriage. If a man decided he wanted to marry one of the girls in the village, he brought her gifts. However, his main concern was winning the approval of her parents and brothers. He would leave venison in front of their door. If they liked the young man, the venison was taken inside as a sign that he was accepted. If they did not take the meat inside, he had not found favor with the girl's family. If a marriage was to take place, the priest was notified, but there was no further marriage ceremony.

When a Caddo Indian died, the size of the ceremony depended on his position within the tribe. Immediately after death, they prepared the body for burial by bathing it carefully and dressing it in fine clothing. If the person was not of high rank in the tribe, the burial might take place within a matter of hours. However, if he was important, such as a priest or shaman, the burial might not be for several days. This gave the entire confederacy time to arrive for the funeral. The body was always buried with the head to the west. Tools and weapons were buried with the men, and useful household cooking vessels were buried with the women. An abundant supply of food was always placed in the grave with the dead.

The Caddoes welcomed strangers into their villages by weeping and wailing. A Spanish or French explorer was usually greeted with a special ceremony and often stayed in the home of the chief. Before entering the chief's home, the priests said prayers and washed the faces of the explorers. The people of the village brought them food and presents.

CRAFTS

The Caddoes were skilled craftsmen. They were well known for their beautiful and long lasting pottery. They were also noted for making reed mats, rugs, and baskets. These were woven in a variety of colors. Early visitors were impressed with the quality workmanship of these crafts.

They used gourds to make rattles for religious ceremonies. Musical instruments were made from bird bones and hollowed-out reeds. They made a drum by stretching deer skin over a hollow log. Sometimes pottery jars, partly filled with water and covered with deer skin, were used as drums.

CHILDREN

As soon as a child was born, the infant was taken to a stream to be washed. In winter months the mother sometimes had to break the ice in order to bathe her child. About a week after the baby's birth, there was a naming ceremony conducted by the priest. The priest came to the parent's home and sat in a place of honor. He talked to the baby and then bathed it in a large vessel. The parents told him the name they had chosen for the baby. This name could be kept throughout the baby's life, or it was sometimes changed to a nickname or a name of one of the spirits.

Boys were forced to bathe in icy streams in order to toughen themselves. They were also taught by the men in the family what to do on a war party. One method of training was to engage in foot races. This was thought to build their endurance and strength. In raising young boys, the relative who helped the most was the boy's uncle. The boy was never to talk back to the uncle; he had to listen to everything the uncle said. When a boy became a skilled hunter, or a successful warrior, he was considered a man and ready for marriage no matter how old he was.

Grandmothers were very important in the training of both boys and girls. She taught them proper behaviors and attitudes, and trained them in the ways of the Caddo people. They learned at an early age to heed their grandmother's teachings.

CONCLUSION

The proud Caddo Indians of East Texas appeared to be economically safe and secure for many years. However, with the coming of the white man, disease and war took their toll on the land and the people.

By the early 1800s only a small remnant of the Caddo people remained in Texas. However, they were probably the most productive and advanced Indians in the state and are best remembered for giving our state its name.

THE WICHITAS

The Wichita (WICH-eh-taw) Indians lived along the Red River, which is the border between Texas and Oklahoma. They settled near present-day Dallas and Fort Worth, and later in the vicinity of Waco. The Wichitas moved southward from Kansas and Oklahoma into Texas to escape the Comanche and Osage Indians.

The tribes and subtribes of the Wichita Indians spoke a common language which made communication between the tribes much easier.

They fought with the Spanish settlers because the Spanish tried to bring the Indians into the Spanish way of life. However, the Wichitas were friendly to the French traders who came into their villages.

The Wichita Indians were short and stocky, and their skin was very dark.

FOOD

The Wichita Indians were primarily farmers. Since they lived along the rivers, rich bottomland produced large fields of maize. The Spaniards, after visiting a Wichita village, agreed that the corn stalks were taller than any they had ever seen. The Wichitas also grew pumpkins, melons, beans, gourds, and squash, and some plum trees could be found in their fields.

Even though the Wichita Indians lived in villages along streams and rivers, fish was not a part of their daily diet. Their main source of meat came from buffalo, which they hunted in the late fall and early winter. They also hunted deer and antelope, and they kept large herds of cattle.

CLOTHING

In the cooler part of the year, Wichita men wore leggings made from fur or skins of the deer and buffalo. They wore a shirt or robe to cover the upper parts of their bodies, and moccasins were worn on their feet. When the weather became warmer, they wore only a loin cloth, also made from skin or fur.

The women wore skirts made from buffalo hide or buckskin. The hide was tanned on both sides to make it softer and more pliable. The skirts were then wound around the women's waists. They were made to reach below their knees. Sometimes they were decorated with elk's teeth, attached to the skirt in rows.

Both men and women tattooed their faces and bodies. The men tattooed both eyelids and were given the name "raccoon-eyed people." They also made two short lines going down from the corners of their mouths. A boy could put a clawlike tattoo on the back of his hand after he killed his first bird. Men also tattooed symbols on their arms and chest to represent war honors, and they pierced their ears in at least four places.

A series of circles, lines, and triangles were tattooed on the women's faces, necks, and arms.

SHELTER

Because the Wichita Indians were farmers, they lived in permanent homes, except when they were on a buffalo hunt. Then they lived in teepees.

The homes of the Wichitas were known as grass

houses and were very strong and sturdy. Using available materials, they made a framework of forked cedar poles. These poles were hammered into the ground in a circle that was fifteen to thirty feet in diameter, depending on how large the house was going to be. Then the poles were bent and tied together at the top. Between these cedar poles the women added willow poles and grasses they had woven together. At the top of the house was a peak with four poles that pointed to the north, south, east, and west. The peak represented the Creator, and the four poles symbolized the gods of all four corners of the earth.

Each house had two low, narrow doors on the east and west side of the house. These doors were made of grass attached to a willow frame. Sometimes a door was also added to the south side of the house and was used for special ceremonies.

In the center of the house was a small hole used for building a fire. A smoke vent was made near the top of the roof. Beds were placed around the walls of the house, raised off the floor, and covered with buffalo hides. The women decorated their houses with curtains made from animal skins. They put paintings on the walls, and made rugs from buffalo hide and deer skin. A large, hollowed-out tree trunk that was sunken into the floor was used for grinding corn.

Each family built an arbor by the side of their house. An arbor looked similar to the house, except all sides were left open and the floor was raised. During the heat of the summer, the family would go there to work or rest.

The Wichitas' homes were strong and warm. Usually, from eight to ten people lived in one house. Since most villages had a thousand or more inhabitants, many of these grass houses could be seen for miles around.

When a house was being built, the head of the family who would live in the house did the hard work of cutting the posts for the frame. All the women of the village helped thatch the grass for the new house. They also prepared food for the workers.

WEAPONS AND TOOLS

Since the Wichita Indians were primarily farmers, their most important tools were crudely made hoes. These were usually made from the bones of a large buffalo and used for planting and caring for their crops.

Pointed sticks were used to scare away birds that invaded their corn fields. An Indian woman would stand on a platform and wave a piece of animal skin and a pointed stick to keep the birds from entering the fields. The platform consisted of four forked poles driven into the ground, with two long poles fitted into the forks of the poles. Then, shorter poles were laid across the two long poles.

They used bows and arrows for hunting wild game. They also used traps for smaller game, such as rabbits, beaver, and coyote. A trap was made by digging a pit and placing bait, such as dead fish, inside. A travois was used to carry their supplies and game.

CUSTOMS AND RELIGION

The Wichitas had small war parties led by warriors in the tribe. It was the leader's custom to choose men for the war party and invite them to his home. There he would explain the plan and make preparations for going on the warpath. A leader was recognized for his brave deeds by pictures drawn on his tepee and clothing. During cold winter evenings, the warriors sat around a campfire and talked about the brave deeds they had done.

A warrior's wife dressed in tattered clothing while her husband was away on the warpath. She did not attend any social gatherings or express any kind of happiness.

If she did, it was believed something would happen to her husband, and he would never return. However, when her husband did return safely from the warpath, the women in her husband's family dressed her in all new clothing. Many days of dancing and parties followed the return of the war party.

The Wichita Indians believed in many gods and goddesses. They divided them into earth and sky, and male and female. They believed everything had a spirit, including plants, trees, and animals. Their most important spirit was called Kinnikasus, whom they believed made the world. This spirit was included in all their prayers. Their sun god, called Man-Reflecting-Light, was also very important. Morning Star was the spirit of the first man created by Kinnikasus. South Star was the guardian of the warriors, and North Star helped guide people on earth. They also feared North Star, since they believed this god brought death, and they often referred to him as Light-Which-Stands-Still. The shaman was given his power from North Star.

Goddesses were also important to the Wichita Indians. Bright Shining Woman watched over the women when they had their babies. Another important goddess was the goddess of water, called Woman-Forever-In-The-Water. She provided the healing power of water for the people and for crops. Earth Mother gave them roots and plants, which were useful in stopping pain and curing those who were sick.

Many of the people belonged to religious societies that performed a variety of chants and dances, led by the shaman. Some of these were done in secret. One dance was called the Calumet Pipe Sticks Dance. During this dance, feathered pipe stems were given to an important person in the tribe. Dances were performed for many occasions, such as harvesting the crops, the return of the war parties, and curing the sick.

They believed in life after death. They were taught that long ago one person had died and returned from the Spirit Land to tell them about the other world.

CHILDREN

When a child was born, an old woman of the tribe took the baby to the river to bathe it. While at the river, the old woman prayed to the moon that the child would grow as quickly as the moon. Then she sprinkled water on the baby's head and prayed to the spirit of the water. The next time the moon appeared the old woman held the baby up to the moon, again asking that the baby grow like the moon.

Many times children were named before they were born. These names may have appeared to the mother in a dream. This caused some children to have names that did not really suit them. Sometimes girls would be given the names of boys, or a boy would have a girl's name. However, a child was usually given a name that was more suitable to his behaviors and actions. If a child was very sickly, he was permitted to choose his own name. The men of the tribe gathered in the father's house and pronouced their names, and the child could choose which name he would prefer. When they became teenagers, they were allowed to change their names if they liked. It was usually changed to that of an older warrior.

The mother and other female relatives provided most of the training and education for the children. Fathers were usually loving to their children, but they were away for several weeks at a time on hunting expeditions or on the warpath.

The children stayed close to their mother for the first few years of their lives. If the baby was not in his mother's arms, he was in a cradle close by. A child was rarely ever spanked by his mother, but was usually disci-

41

plined by scolding. If an older child became difficult to handle, the mother might call in an older person to help with the discipline. This was usually someone who was not related to the child, and he would threaten the child with many things, such as throwing him in the creek or pretending to eat him up.

Fathers had more influence in a boy's life as he grew older. It was important that the boys learn to be brave and strong. They were taught how to hunt, ride a horse, and engage in the games of the tribe.

The girls were taught to do the household chores like gardening and sewing. They were often married before they were sixteen years of age.

The Wichita children learned about their gods from a storyteller. He was invited to the house and asked to teach the children about the spirits. The storyteller taught them that everything, including trees, animals, and people had a spirit. He taught them how the world began with the creation of the first man and woman, who had been given bows and arrows and an ear of corn. They learned how the people were scattered over the earth, went through a period of wrongdoing, and suffered through a terrible flood. The storyteller taught them about life after death and the belief that all the stars and the sun would become human again.

CONCLUSION

The Wichita Indians were caught between two great forces, the Plains Indians and the white man. They were brave warriors who fought to hold on to their land. Unfortunately, early Ango-American settlers forced the Wichitas to give up their homeland.

Plagued by disease and war, many of the Wichita Indians died. Those who survived were moved to reservations. By the mid-1800s, most of the Wichitas were gone from Texas. Many of their descendents now live in the neighboring state of Oklahoma.

The Atakapans

The Atakapans (ah-TACK-keh-pans) came to Texas from Louisiana, and they settled along the northern part of the Gulf Coast. Their lands stretched from Louisiana across the Sabine River and as far as the Trinity and San Jacinto rivers. Two of their villages were located on either side of the Neches River near present-day Beaumont. They were also known as Atakapas, and their name meant "river people."

The marshy land of the Atakapan Indians was not suitable for growing crops. Much of the land was flooded with salt water, and some were forced to move inland. The more wooded areas provided wild game for their food supply. Deer, bear, and bison were plentiful in this area.

It is believed that one of the coastal tribes of the Atakapans, as well as the Karankawas, came in contact with the Spanish explorer, Cabeza de Vaca. The French explorer La Salle passed through their lands but had little to say about the Atakapans.

FOOD

The main source of food for the Atakapans came from hunting and fishing. With their pirogues, or dugout canoes, they fished along the Gulf Coast. Their canoes were not very sturdy, so they did not go far out into the

43

Gulf. They rarely used a bow and arrow for fishing, but they used a spear or darts instead. They were very accurate with their bone-tipped spears and darts that had been tipped with many sharp fish bones.

Another method of fishing used by the Atakapans was to use pieces of brushwood to block off a shallow part of the Gulf and trap the fish inside.

After the day's catch, most of the fish was smoked for later use. The fish that were to be eaten that day were cleaned and baked in an open pit.

Oysters were also a part of the Atakapans' diet and were plentiful on the Gulf Coast. Alligators became another source of food. Alligator oil was used on their skin to keep the mosquitoes away. They also ate clams, scallops, turtles, and wild plants that grew underneath the water.

The Atakapans who lived further inland were able to raise some crops, such as corn, beans, squash, and tobacco.

Deer was plentiful and therefore was the most frequently hunted animal. Hunters traveled to the western prairies to hunt buffalo. They also hunted bear for their skin and fat. It is believed they did not eat the meat of the bear.

They also gathered berries, seeds, and nuts. These were eaten alone or cooked in a meat stew.

CLOTHING

The Atakapan Indians were short and stout, and their heads were large compared to the rest of their bodies. Their mouths and ears were very large, and they had high cheekbones and protruding lips.

Some Atakapan tribes are said to have practiced head flattening. They did this by padding a thin board with moss and material and tying it to a baby's head for a year. This caused the child's head to slope and become slanted. The Atakapans considered this shaping of the head to be a thing of beauty. Their hair was cut short and was coarse and bushy. They used a variety of leaves for tobacco, causing their teeth to be stained.

The Atakapans tattooed their face and body, and they sometimes put cuts on their nose and chin. The men of the tribe went barefoot, and their main article of clothing in the summer was a breechcloth. When the weather turned colder, they added a robe made of buffalo skin. The robe was usually painted on the inside with red and black geometric designs. Sometimes the tail of the buffalo was left on the robe and trailed behind. The men also stuck large hooped earrings through their pierced ears.

The dress of the Atakapan women was very simple. A skin was placed on the ground and cut into a circle. Then a hole was cut in the center of the circle, so the dress could be easily slipped over her head. A shawl of Spanish moss was sometimes draped across her shoulder.

SHELTER

The homes of the Atakapans had to be easy to take apart and carry. They were made of willow poles that were interwoven with vines. The cone-shaped top was left open for the smoke to escape. Their fireplace was made of oyster shells and placed in the middle of the dirt floor. They often built these huts on old shell heaps called "middens."

The huts of the shaman and those that were head of the village were placed on higher ground, usually on the very top of a shell heap.

WEAPONS AND TOOLS

Primarily fishermen, the Atakapans used spears and darts for fishing. They were tipped with sharp fish bones. They used rakes made of two strong poles curved on the end and wrapped with strong vines to "drag" oysters from the bottom of the Gulf.

Small animals, such as rabbits and squirrels, were caught in traps made of cane. They also used bow and arrows to hunt buffalo, deer, and bear.

CUSTOMS AND RELIGION

The Atakapan Indians were divided into at least four bands, and each band had its own chief. There was no tribal chief over all the bands.

Like the Caddoes, the Atakapans followed the custom of "wailing" or crying when they greeted a visitor. A visitor could easily become frightened by this behavior unless he knew their crying was for joy as well as for sadness.

It was the woman's task to build the mound on which the chief's house would be built. She also took charge of the fields and the household. The job of the men was to supply meat for the village.

Ceremonial dances were performed by the Atakapans. Their dances were very noisy and wild, as they leaped and yelled around large bonfires. Only the men were allowed to dance. The women had to stand some distance away from the fire, where they could join in the singing part of the ceremony. These ceremonial dances sometimes lasted several days. They danced and sang until they became too exhausted to continue.

They believed their people came out of the sea, and a man of God called a prophet wrote rules on how they should conduct themselves. To their way of thinking, "a person who goes about doing good things will go above, and those who go about doing evil things will go below." However, if a man died from a snake bite, he could not enter a second life. The religious leader of the Atakapans was the shaman. He also served as their doctor, preparing roots and herbs to cure the sick.

CHILDREN

The children were born in huts that had been specially built for that purpose. The mother was helped by several older women of the village. When the baby was born, it was strapped to a piece of bark that had been bent so it fit the body of the baby. Only the head was left free. The child was released from this bark cage twice each day.

When a boy baby was born, the father of the child changed his name. This practice was called "teknonymy." The man became known as the father of so-and-so (the child's name). If the child died, the father took back his old name.

CONCLUSION

Although we know very little about the Atakapans, we find they had a very interesting culture. They were a small tribe compared to some of the other Texas tribes. They probably did not number more than 3,500 people. The tribes along the Gulf Coast had a different culture and language and found it impossible to live with their relatives who lived further into the interior of Texas.

A few Atakapans were known to be living in Texas as late as 1885.

The Tonkawas

The Tonkawa (TONG-keh-wah) Indians lived on the lands of the Edwards Plateau near present-day Austin. Some bands lived on the Coastal Plains to the south and along the Brazos river bottoms to the east.

The name Tonkawa means "they all stay together." They referred to themselves as "the most human of people." When the scattered bands of Tonkawas became smaller in number in the early 1800s, those that remained united into one tribe.

Archeological sites of the Tonkawa Indians have been found along the streams and rivers of Central Texas. They often camped on burnt rock middans of the Edwards Plateau. Remains of plain pottery made by these Indians have been found, as well as pottery they obtained from Caddo tribes.

Some of La Salle's followers met Indians thought to be Tonkawas. These Indians invited the French explorers to their village, but the French were not going in that direction and did not accept their invitation.

During Alonso de Leon's expedition in 1690, the first accounts written by the Europeans about the Tonkawas was recorded. When the Spanish explorers came near the Tonkawa camps, the Indians ran for the woods, leaving behind their dogs, already packed with buffalo hides.

The Tonkawa Indians requested that missions be established and several were built for them in the early eighteenth century. It is almost certain they did not ask for these missions for any religious purpose, but for safety from European invaders.

FOOD

The Tonkawas depended on the buffalo for most of their food supply even though only a few herds roamed through their hunting grounds. They would have left the Edwards Plateau region and moved to the more abundant buffalo plains to the north and west if it had been possible. However, this land was already claimed by the Apaches and Comanches, and they would not allow the Tonkawas to invade their land.

Deer became very important to the Tonkawa Indians, not only for food but for hides that could be traded to white settlers.

They hunted skunks, rats, rabbits, bear, and land tortoises for food. The Tonkawas were especially fond of rattlesnake meat; however, they never ate wolves or coyotes. These animals were considered to be sacred and were a part of their religious beliefs.

Unlike other Plains Indian tribes, the Tonkawas ate fish and oysters. It is believed they got the seafood by trading with coastal tribes or on trips made to the Gulf of Mexico.

These nomadic Indians even tried farming but found it to be unsuccessful. So, they ate a variety of fruit, seeds, herbs, and roots. They gathered acorns, pecans, and prickly pear. Pecans became particularly important to the Tonkawas because they were able to barter, or trade them to the settlers.

They prepared the meat of the buffalo and deer by roasting it over an open fire. Any meat that was not eaten immediately was preserved into jerky or pemmican. They not only pounded berries into the meat but also meal made from pecans. A length of intestine from one of the animals was then stuffed into the mixture. The jerky or pemmican could be easily taken on hunting expeditions.

SHELTER

As long as the buffalo were plentiful, the Tonkawa Indians lived in tepees. They were short, crudely made dwellings, which never compared to the tall, impressive tepees of the northern Plains Indians. Additional buildings, used when a mother gave birth to a child or for ceremonial dances, were made of brush. They were low, round huts shaped like a dome and made from willow saplings. Grass, hides, brush, or any other available material covered the saplings.

When the Apache and Comanche tribes made it impossible for the Tonkawas to hunt on their land, buffalo became very scarce. Soon, they were forced to use the dome-shaped huts as their permanent dwellings.

WEAPONS AND TOOLS

The Tonkawa Indians had few tools or weapons, and those they had were very crudely made. Their most important weapon was the bow and arrow. For many years they used stone-tipped arrows, but when metal was traded to them by the Europeans they made metal-tipped arrows instead. They used the juice of mistletoe on the arrow tips because they thought mistletoe was poison. Later, after obtaining guns from the white man, they continued to use mistletoe juice, placing it inside the barrel of their guns.

Lances, weapons with long shafts and sharp metal heads, were used in battle and for hunting wild game. Shields, helmets, and jackets were made from the hide of the buffalo.

Most of their other tools and weapons came from the buffalo. From the hoofs of the buffalo they made glue used in making their arrows. Sinew, tendon from the buffalo, was used to make thread for sewing and strings for their bows. When ropes were needed, the Tonkawas made them from the tail of the buffalo, and spoons and cups were carved from the buffalo's horns.

The Tonkawas made some pottery and some of it was obtained from the Caddo Indians in East Texas. They used the bark of mulberry trees to make a crude type of cloth. They made baskets and mats by weaving grasses and other fibres together.

CUSTOMS AND RELIGION

The Tonkawa Indians lived in small bands for many years. Each tribe had its own chief, and in times of war a special war chief was chosen. Later, when the bands joined together to form a tribe, each band continued to have its own chief, but a head chief was chosen to govern the entire tribe. By banding together as a tribe the Tonkawas were able to gain strength in numbers, and when it became necessary for them to be at war with their enemies, they had a better chance for survival. When a chief died, the men of the tribe gathered together to choose who would be the next chief.

The tribe was split into two separate groups of totemic clans. A totemic clan was a clan composed of relatives who could trace their heritage back to some mythical ancestor. Each clan had a special name, such as buffalo, bear, mouth open, short snake, or acorn. Children were born into the clan of their mother rather than their father. When the two clans met for a council meeting, they sat on opposite sides of the council fire.

Clan members lived together and helped each other in their daily activities. When a man of the clan died, he was buried with many of his possessions. The possessions that were not buried with him were not given to his own children, but to the children of his brother or sister.

There are no records of how or when the Tonkawa Indians were married. It is supposed the marriage ceremony was not their most important concern. However, death was treated with a great deal of ceremony. When a person was thought to be dying, relatives and friends came to his tepee. Some of them formed a circle around him and placed their hands upon his body. Others formed another circle, placing their hands upon the shoulders of those in the first circle. They began to sway and chant, and they stayed with the dying person throughout the night.

When a person died, he was buried immediately unless he was the chief. Chiefs might not be buried for several days so all the people would have an opportunity to see him one more time. The face of the deceased was painted yellow, his hair cut, and the body wrapped in his best buffalo robe. Relatives and friends did not eat until after the burial had taken place. They came to the burial place with gifts that were to be buried with the body. These gifts, such as guns, clothing, and saddles, were placed in the grave with the body. If it was the death of a woman of the tribe, the beads from her clothing were removed and buried with her. The ashes of a dead man's pipes were hidden away forever, and some of his other possessions were burned. Sometimes a favorite horse or dog was shot over his grave.

For three days after the burial the friends and relatives of the deceased mourned. No singing or chanting was allowed during this period of mourning. The entire clan joined the relatives with long periods of crying and wailing at sunrise and again at dusk. At the end of the mourning period the chief spoke to the people, and from that point on, the deceased person's name was never spoken again. They believed if the names of the dead were spoken, it would anger his spirit, and he might come back to bother those that were still living. After the chief had spoken to the people, they performed a four-day smoking ceremony. It was led by the shaman, and the people talked quietly and blew smoke toward the sky. Friends and relatives also brought gifts of food, clothing and other items, replacing those that had been burned or buried at the funeral.

The shaman was the medicine man and religious leader of the tribe. During a medicine dance, a special tepee was built facing east. There was a small hole dug in the center of the tepee where a fire was built. The sick person came into the tepee, walked around the fire on the south side and sat on a blanket that was spread on the ground. The shaman then began the curing ceremony by rubbing parts of the patient's body that needed to be cured. He applied medicines and called to some supernatural being to provide a cure for his patient. When the shaman had completed the ceremony, the patient left the tepee the same way he had entered.

The Tonkawa Indians believed there were supernatural gods and that the most important one was the spirit of the dead. Since they believed these spirits traveled to the west, they always buried their people with their heads placed toward the west. Those who were living always slept with their feet pointed toward the west for fear their soul might start its journey too soon.

They believed a woman's soul went directly home to the west, singing as it went. However, the soul of a man stayed around awhile to watch their living relatives. These spirits took the form of owls and wolves and the Tonkawas would not kill these animals. Certain places would not be visited at night. They believed that strange sounds heard in these places were sounds of the dead, and if these spirits visited them they too would soon die.

CHILDREN

Before a Tonkawa baby was born the father could not touch any kind of bird. It was believed if he did this the child would be born with weak legs. The baby was born in a special brush hut. A day after the child was born the mother bathed in a stream and applied white clay to her face. The mother and father of the new baby were not allowed to smoke or use any kind of firearms for four days after the birth. They believed any kind of smoke would cause the baby to have weak eyes.

Babies were placed on a cradleboard soon after birth, and its head was flattened by tying a piece of wood to it. After it was about eighteen months old, it was allowed to leave the cradleboard and move around the camp. The child was not given a name until it was several years old. Children were seldom punished by their parents. One method of punishment was to throw water on the offender.

Children learned their duties and what was expected of them from their parents. A child of divorced parents or an orphan was cared for by members of their mother's clan.

CONCLUSION

Today the Tonkawa Indians are an almost forgotten people. Perhaps, since these timid people were not adept at warfare, they were simply overlooked by most of the early Texans.

The Tonkawas were caught between the advance of the white man on the east and the aggressive Comanches on the west. Their tribes began to decline and the people scattered, some settling in Mexico. The existence of the Tonkawas as a separate people came to an end about 1850.

The Kiowas

The Kiowa (KYE-eh-wah) Indians migrated south from Montana and Wyoming about three hundred years ago, settling on the plains of Kansas and Oklahoma. In the late 1700s and early 1800s, about 2,000 Kiowas moved to the Panhandle of Texas. The area east and north of present-day Amarillo became their home.

The Kiowas became great warriors and horsemen in this dry Texas grassland. Like other Plains Indians they were prepared to move quickly and often. They shared a friendship with the Wichita Indians and traded with them often.

FOOD

Buffalo was the main source of food for the Kiowa Indians. Their buffalo hunts were more organized than other Indian tribes. Warrior societies, a type of police group, were organized to keep hunters from killing buffalo that were not needed. They found the buffalo herds, surrounded them, and stood guard while the hunters killed the encircled animals. Sometimes the buffalo herd would run at full force, or stampede, and be driven over the cliffs. Indians waited below to shoot or spear those buffalo that were not killed in the fall.

Other animals, such as antelope, deer, and rabbits were another source of food. They would not eat dogs, coyotes, wild birds, or fish unless they were starving. They killed bear for its fat, which was used to season their food.

The Kiowas used the "surround" method of hunting antelope. The antelope were penned in a corral made of logs. At the opening of the corral two scarecrow posts covered with blankets were set up. The antelope were driven through this opening. Then the medicine man came to perform his ceremony. He directed the mounted hunters to form a large semicircle. They slowly moved toward the women and children who completed the circle. No shooting was allowed within the surround. Hunters used their hands or ropes to capture the animal. Only if the animal escaped could he be shot.

Pitfalls for trapping antelope were sometimes hidden along the trails.

The Kiowa did not raise crops, but were able to trade with other Indians for these products. They ate a variety of fruits, berries, wild plants, nuts, and roots.

Stew, made from pemmican mixed with berries and nuts, was a favorite of the Kiowa Indians. A favorite desert was bits of pemmican covered with honey.

They sometimes drank the warm blood of a freshly killed animal because they believed it was healthy for them.

CLOTHING

During the summer months, Kiowa men wore a breechcloth which was attached to their belts and hung to their knees. They wore deerskin moccasins when it was warm. In colder weather they added leggings made of tanned buffalo hide or deerskin. These leggings covered their body from the hip to the feet and were usually decorated with shells, animal teeth, and beads. They also wore V-necked shirts made from the skins of buffalo, deer, or antelope. During a winter storm, warm buffalo robes and snowshoes were also added.

Kiowa women wore high moccasins to protect their legs from the wind and cold of the Texas Plains. They also wore dresses made of deerskin.

Clothing worn by the war parties was very elaborate. The warriors enjoyed wearing headdresses made of bird feathers. Many of their headdresses were decorated with the horns of a cow.

A Kiowa warrior cut his hair short on the right side to show off a variety of ear ornaments. He let the hair on his left side grow as long as possible. The long hair was wrapped or tied in a loop with a piece of deer sinew. A scalp lock was left hanging down his back.

The Kiowa women parted their hair in the middle. Many allowed the hair to fall free, with only a headband to secure it in place. Others plaited their hair into two long braids, which they tied at the end with deerskin.

Both men and women were fond of any kind of metal ornaments. They decorated their clothing and bodies with silver. Metal trinkets were also attached to their horses.

SHELTER

The Kiowa, like other Indians of the plains, had to move quickly and often in search of buffalo. They lived in tepees made of tanned hides. These tepees were built on a four-pole foundation to which twenty additional poles were added to complete the frame. As many as twenty hides, depending on the size of the tepee, were sewn together and fastened around the framework. These hides were all decorated with beautiful paintings. Pegs were used to fasten the hides at the bottom. The entrance to the tepee was three or four feet high and was slightly raised off the ground. It faced the east so the sun could enter the tepee during the morning. The entrance was closed with a stiff piece of animal skin. It was fastened with buckskin strings so that it would close by itself on windy days. When the weather was warm, the sides could be rolled up to enjoy the summer breezes.

A fire pit was dug in the center of the tepee. Along the sides away from the door they placed their beds. These were made from willow rods placed across poles. Animal skins and blankets were thrown across the top of the beds. When they were not used for sleeping, they were used as a place to sit. The entrance side of the tepee was used as the kitchen and for storage.

WEAPONS AND TOOLS

The few possessions of the Kiowa Indians needed to be durable and easy to move. They had no pottery or baskets, but made containers of tanned animal skins. Spoons and utensils were made from animal horns.

Their main weapons were bows and arrows and lances. Their arrow cases or quivers were never made of deer, antelope, or buffalo skin unless it was absolutely necessary. They liked to use panther skin or Mexican leather. Later, when they were able to obtain firearms from the white man, guns were used. However, they never abandoned the use of lances or bows and arrows.

CUSTOMS AND RELIGION

The Kiowas took great pride in their ceremonies and traditions. They kept journals of their travels and painted pictures on buffalo hide to record important events in their lives.

A newly-married couple usually lived with the husband's family. Only if the man was poor or of low rank in the tribe did they live with the family of the girl. The men sometimes had several wives to help with the many chores of the tribe.

After a buffalo was killed, it was the woman's job to skin and butcher the animal, pack the meat on horses, and take it back to camp. She prepared the meat for eating and made jerky for future use. The women erected the tepees when the Kiowas settled in a new location and dismantled them when it was time to move. They cared for the children and did other household chores.

Within the Kiowa tribe there were six warrior societies. These societies included all the male members of the tribe. Each society had two leaders and two sergeants-at-arms, who kept the behavior of the members under control. They also had their own dances, songs, and duties.

Membership in the highest military society was reserved for only the bravest warriors of the tribe. Their duty was to lead in the most dangerous battles, and they were never to retreat. The leader wore an elk skin sash around his neck which hung to the ground on his right side. During a battle, he had to dismount in front of his warriors and throw a ceremonial arrow through the elk skin and into the ground. He stayed in this spot until the battle was over. If his warriors were defeated and forced to retreat, members of his society would pull the arrow out of the ground and free the leader. However, if the leader was killed during the battle, another leader was chosen to take his place. When the sash-owner became too old to go to battle, the sash was passed to another warrior.

The most important duty of the Kiowa societies was to oversee the Sun Dance. This festival was usually held in midsummer just before the great buffalo hunts which took place in the fall. One of the tribal chiefs was chosen as the religious leader for the Sun Dance. He picked the location for the dance. It had to be held where there was a large supply of wood for cooking, water for people and animals, and grass for the horses. After the chief decided on a site, he told a number of young braves, who were sent to tell all the families of the tribe. The people were told long before the Sun Dance was to take place because the Kiowas believed sacred things should be done slowly.

The Sun Dance festival lasted about twelve days. The first four days were spent traveling and setting up tepees. For the Sun Dance, the tepees were placed in a large circle. The openings of the tepees always faced the center of the circle.

The next four days were called Getting Ready Time. During these four days the ceremonial lodge was built. A large, tall tree trunk was placed in the center. Smaller logs made the lodge walls, and these were covered with green willow branches. During the Getting Ready Time, feasts, games, and sports competitions were held.

During the last four days, the Sun Dance was performed. During the dance, the braves danced around the center pole of the lodge for many hours, sticking sharp sticks into their bodies. They could show no pain no matter how much they suffered. The Sun Dance was a symbol of the struggle of the soul to free itself from the bonds of the body. The Kiowas proudly displayed the scars of the Sun Dance as though they were badges of honor.

There were other religious societies among the Kiowa Indians. One was a society for great warriors, known as the Crazy Dogs. The Buffalo Doctors was a society that treated diseases and wounds involving blood. Eagle Shields was led by a shaman who treated diseases by using his magical powers.

There were only two societies for the women of the tribe. One society, called the Calf Old Women, could only be joined by invitation, and only the old women of the tribe were allowed to become members. They had feasts and were allowed to dance as part of the Sun Dance. The other society for women was called The Bear Women, and since it was a secret society little is known about its activities.

The Kiowa buried their dead in high places, and

their equipment and possessions were buried with them or burned. A warrior's horse was killed over the grave. Women in mourning cut their hair close to their heads and cut gashes in their faces and arms. Men mourned the loss of a loved one by cutting their hair to shoulder length. They also put away their fine clothes and ornaments.

Kiowa war parties covered a large area of land. They were known to have gone to the northern plains, the western border of New Mexico, and as far south as British Honduras. These long raids were made on horseback, while shorter raids were taken on foot. To obtain warriors for a large war party the ceremony of "giving the pipe" was performed. This was done during the Sun Dance when a warrior sent a pipe to each of the leaders of the warrior societies. If they wished to join the war party, the pipe was smoked. The pipe was not smoked for smaller war parties.

The leader asked other warriors to join him, and the night before leaving for war he bent a stick in the shape of a hoop, placing it around the fire in his tepee. Then he began to sing a song of travel as he beat the hoop with a stick. Those warriors who wished to join him came into the tepee and began to beat time on the hoop with him. Women entered the tepee later, sat behind the men, and sang.

A raid was thought to be successful if none of the warriors were killed. If no one was lost and the war party returned with horses, scalps and other possessions, there was a great celebration. The warriors, with their faces painted black to show they had defeated the enemy, entered the camp at full speed firing guns and shooting their bows and arrows. They took the women up on their horses with them and rode around in a circle singing. At night they built a fire and the warriors and the women all danced. Sometimes these dances were held every afternoon and night for an entire month.

A Kiowa became a warrior by performing four deeds of bravery or skill. He loved to brag about his war deeds, and did so at every opportunity.

Even though the Kiowa were involved in many raids and attacks, they were not always the aggressors. They were known to have been attacked by the Arapahoes, Osage, and Cheyenne tribes.

The Kiowas believed there were many gods, with the main god being the sun. They believed all plants and animals had more than normal powers. Owls and other nocturnal birds were thought to possess the souls of the dead. Dreams and visions were taken very seriously and could sometimes be the deciding point on whether a warrior went on a raid or a hunt.

One of their religious beliefs involved medicine bundles called the Ten Grandmothers. Each person had a bundle. These bundles were used for prayer and sometimes sacrifice. The Ten Grandmothers were well cared for. Each bundle was guarded by a trusted family member who gave them sweat baths and made sure the containers were always in good repair. Once a year the bundles were brought to the priest who opened them in his ceremonial tepee. He purified them with smoke before they were returned to the guardian.

The Kiowas used pictographs, usually on buffalo skin, to make up calendars of important events in the tribe. They started at the lower right-hand corner of the hide and ended near the center. Black bars were drawn to signify winter and a drawing of the medicine lodge was used to show summer. The important events that had taken place during the year were placed beside the appropriate season. In this manner an account of their history was made. During the long winter nights, warriors would gather in a tepee to share the pipe and tell some great deed of war, a tribal tradition, or some event that had taken place in their lives.

It was believed by the Kiowas that there was one omnipotent being who created the world. After this creation, he traveled to the west until he found a hollow tree lying on the ground. He pretended to hit the tree three times, and on the fourth time he hit it with full force and out came the Kiowas, who were frightened and ran away. He called to them and told them they were his children. Then he noticed that some were not correctly put together so he corrected their flaws and sent them on their way. He hit the log again and more grown men and women came out and they too ran away. He called them back, and since they were all perfectly formed he sent them on their way. He hit the tree a third time and this time both children and adults came out. He gave the Kiowas their tools and weapons and told them how they were to be used.

Then, according to the Kiowa legend, the omnipotent one met the Great White Man. He returned to the Kiowas and told them they were to treat the white men who came to their land as enemies. The creator then became a group of stars.

CHILDREN

Usually children were named soon after they were born by a grandparent or some other close relative. Sometimes an important man of the tribe would name the child and the family would give him gifts of horses and buffalo hides for providing the baby's name. Children were sometimes named for some great deed by their ancestors or some important family event. Later, boys sometimes changed their names to fit some action they had shown during the hunt or on the warpath. Older men, sometimes close to the end of their lives, would give their names to a younger warrior. They would choose a new name for themselves or remain nameless until their death. Names of the dead were never used again.

Boys belonged to a group called the Rabbit Society. They were drilled by two older men of the tribe and instructed on how to become a warrior. It was the only kind of school the boys ever attended. The Rabbit Society had feasts where they danced and hopped like rabbits. They wore a piece of elk hide on the back of their heads. The hair of the elk was left on and a feather was placed upright in the elk hide. This was a symbol of their society. Boys stayed in the society until they were old enough to be asked to join one of the older warrior groups.

As boys grew older they were asked to join war parties. They did not engage in battles at first, but they went with the older warriors to herd the horses. Later they were able to join in the raids. It was also during this time a Kiowa boy found it necessary to form a relationship with supernatural beings. He would sometimes go to a hill or mesa to pray, smoke, or fast and wait for a vision. The vision was to show him direction for his life and show him songs to sing and symbols to paint. Sometimes he would have a vision and other times he would not.

Girls could be married by the time they were fourteen, and boys were sometimes married at sixteen. The boy gave the girl's parents gifts of horses and other possessions in return for the loss of their daughter. If an agreement was made between the parents and the boy, the couple could be married.

CONCLUSION

The Kiowa Indians fought to preserve their way of life. However, diseases brought by the white man and battles with other Indian tribes proved to be too much for these Indians of the plains.

Those that remained were forced to live on reservations. By the early 1900s there were few Kiowa Indians left in Texas, but they left behind a rich history of their customs, traditions, and nomadic way of life.

LONE WOLF

Lone Wolf was an important chief of the Kiowa Indians. Many Kiowas had been placed on a reservation in Oklahoma and Lone Wolf seemed to have a good relationship with the army.

However, Lone Wolf felt a deep hatred of the Texans. He believed they were driving the buffalo west, where they were slaughtered by hunters who sold their hides. He believed the buffalo would be totally destroyed unless the Texans were driven away.

Lone Wolf led a band of warriors into Texas in a series of raids. The braves returned with over two hundred horses and mules and other possessions of the white settlers.

Lone Wolf came to the army many times to offer his friendship. While he visited with the army officials, his braves went on raiding parties to Texas. When the army became suspicious of who was responsible for the raids, Lone Wolf brought his braves with him to offer their friendship. While they talked, small groups would slip away to Texas and continue raiding the settlers.

In 1873, one of Lone Wolf's warriors took nine Kiowas and twenty Comanches to the Nueces River where they built a hideaway camp. They sneaked into Mexico, raided a village, and captured two young boys. News reached the army about the raid, and when the Kiowas returned to Texas with a large herd of stolen cattle they were stopped by the United States Army and chased back to Indian Territory in Oklahoma.

When those that survived reached Lone Wolf's camp, the chief was so upset he burned most of his belongings, cut off his hair, and killed his best horses. Then he began to plan his revenge. He and his braves made one more minor raid before they were forced to hide in a mountain cave to escape the army.

Finally, in 1875, Lone Wolf and his braves surrendered. He was put in a Florida prison for three years. By the time he was released he was ill with malaria. Lone Wolf died in 1879.

MAMAN-TI

Maman-ti was born about 1835. When he was young he became a medicine man for the Kiowa Indians. He loved to listen to the sound of the screech-owl and began to study and understand its language. Because he learned new sources of medicine from this bird, he became known as the prophet of the owl.

He had several children by two different wives. He also raised a white boy called Tejan. Even though Tejan had bright red hair and none of the features of an Indian, he was treated as one of the family.

Maman-ti had the ability to predict the outcome of battles, even knowing how many warriors would be killed. Because he was so accurate with his predictions he made the decisions on when and how a battle would be fought.

The night before a battle Maman-ti would meet with the chiefs. An owl was placed on Maman-ti's wrist, and he would talk with the bird and explain to the chiefs what the bird was saying. The chiefs believed that Maman-ti's deceased ancestors were speaking words of wisdom to him through the owl.

An example of his ability to tell the future was in the Lost Valley raid into Texas, led by Maman-ti. The night before the raid he told the chiefs no Indians would die during the battle, two of the white settlers would die, and the heroes of the battle would be riding gray horses. The battle happened just as he said, with two young braves on gray horses capturing more horses and possessions than any others in the war party.

Maman-ti, the Owl Prophet, was an active participant in all battles. He put on warpaint like the others and lead many of the raids himself. When he went into battle, he was stripped to the waist, his body painted white all over and decorated with blue owls painted on his back and chest. His horse was also painted in this manner and decorated with a red cloth.

In 1874, Maman-ti and his braves went to Anadarko, Indian Territory in Oklahoma, where several skirmishes occurred with army troops. The Indians were scattered by the troops and many of them surrendered. The remainder fled to a hiding place on the Texas Plains. The hiding place, unknown to the white man, was Palo Duro Canyon. Maman-ti assured his men the canyon was a safe refuge from the army.

Scouts from the army found the hiding place and conducted a surprise raid on the Kiowas. Most of their horses were captured or destroyed.

Maman-ti was put in shackles and sent to prison in Florida. Three months later he called friends to his prison room where he told them he would die three hours after sunup. The next morning he asked them to return, said farewell to each of them, and lay down on his cot and died.

SATANTA

The name Satanta brought fear to the white settlers in Oklahoma and Texas. The Kiowas, however, associated his name with leadership and courage.

Satanta, called White Bear, was born about 1830 in Indian Territory. He was raised as a warrior and was involved in many battles with the settlers and other Indian tribes.

In 1840, a smallpox epidemic spread through the tribes and many Kiowas died from the dreaded disease. Satanta lost many friends and family to this illness.

Satanta led many raids into Texas long after the Kiowas had made peace with the United States Army.

On one raiding party into Texas he captured a woman and her four children and tried to get the United States to pay a ransom for their return. The United States refused to pay the ransom and demanded they be returned. Satanta said he would have to discuss it with the other chiefs, but instead the war party slipped away with the captives. They later traded them to the army at Fort Dodge for the money they were asking.

Peace treaties were signed between the Kiowas and the army and Satanta became popular with the army leaders. However, even after the Kiowas were settled on reservations, they continued their raids into Texas.

After several skirmishes, battles, and raids on the white settlers Satanta was sent to Texas to stand trial. The United States stated that Satanta and his braves must return all the stolen wagons and mules they had taken in the raids. Satanta started to draw his pistol, stating that he had rather die than stand trial, but realized he was surrounded by armed soldiers of the United States.

Satanta was taken to Fort Richardson where he was condemned to die by hanging. The governor of Texas commuted his sentence to life in prison instead. After two years, he was released on condition that the Kiowas would conduct no more raids in Texas.

When more raids did occur in Texas, it was believed that Satanta was involved. Actually, he had become a buffalo hunter instead. However, he was arrested and put back in prison. He became so depressed he felt a need to end his unhappy existence. On October 11, 1878, Satanta dived headfirst from the upper story of his prison hospital room and died.

The Comanches

The Comanche (coe-MAHN-chee) Indians came to Texas from their homeland in the Rocky Mountains. They settled in the northern and western areas of Texas, hunting large herds of buffalo that roamed the open plains. Their land, which was known as the comancheria (ko-mahn-cheh-REE-ah), extended from the Cross Timbers west to the Pecos River and northward from the Edwards Plateau into Oklahoma and Kansas.

The Comanches came to Texas in family groups and bands. There were as many as twelve different bands of Comanches living in Texas at one time. The largest band was known as the Honey-Eaters, and one of the most nomadic bands was called the Wanderers.

Comanche warriors obtained horses from the Spanish explorers in the 1600s. They became expert horsemen, which gave them a great advantage during a buffalo hunt or in battle. With the speed of the horse and the ability of the riders, the Comanches were able to raid settlers' homes and drive other Indians from the land. They were greatly feared by the homesteaders and other Indian tribes.

The wealth of a Comanche Indian depended on how many horses he owned. He would sometimes offer a horse as a gift to his new bride. Horses were also used in payment for a shaman's help or other means of exchange. Some of the wealthier Comanches owned as many as 1,000 or more horses. These were obtained by stealing from the settlers, trading, or capturing wild mustangs at water holes and on the open plain.

FOOD

Buffalo was the most important food for the nomadic Comanche Indians. Large buffalo hunts were usually conducted in the summer when the animals were fatter and in the fall when the hides were thicker. When an Indian scout spotted a large herd of buffalo, the Comanches set up camp close to the herd and near a stream. A hunt leader was chosen and each hunter knew what he was expected to do. The hunters rode toward the buffalo downwind and slowly circled the herd. As they rode around the herd, the buffalo moved closer and closer together, making it easier for the kill. They shot the animals from the right side so it would enter the heart and kill the animal quickly. If this surround method was unsuccessful, the hunters took advantage of the buffalo's poor eyesight and stampeded them off the side of a cliff. Those that were not killed in the fall were shot or speared by Indians waiting below.

After the kill, fresh meat was enjoyed by members of the band. Sometimes the meat was boiled and made into a stew. Meat that was not eaten immediately was cut into long strips and hung up to dry. Later, wild berries and fat were pounded into the buffalo strips to make pemmican for use during the long winter months. Since pemmican could be preserved for long periods of time, was highly nutritious and easy to carry, it was the best food to take with them as they followed the buffalo. The meat was packed in a rectangular shaped box called a parfleche. It was made from buffalo hide and decorated with brightly-colored designs.

Other sources of food for the Comanches included

elk, grizzly bears, wolves, and antelope. Occasionally Longhorn cattle, stolen from the Texas settlers, were also eaten. Comanches would not eat fish or fowl unless it was absolutely necessary.

They added grapes, berries, persimmons, pecans, acorns, plums, and some tubers and roots to their diet when they were available. Since Comanches did not farm, they traded with other Indian tribes for corn.

Usually the Comanches ate very little in the morning. They ate whenever they were hungry during the day and consumed their heaviest meal in the evening. No matter what time of day or night when a visitor arrived in the Comanche's camp, he was always offered food.

CLOTHING

Most clothing worn by the Comanche Indians came from the buffalo. The women wore loose-fitting blouses and long, uneven skirts made from soft buffalo hide. These were usually trimmed with colorful beads and fringe. They wore moccasins when it was warm, but added leggings and knee-high boots during the cold winter months.

The women wore their hair parted in the middle and cut very short. The appearance of their hair seemed to be of no importance to them. However, a Comanche squaw spent a great deal of time applying a variety of paints to her face. She highlighted her eyes with streaks of red and yellow above and below her eyelids. She painted the inside of her ears red and made a red-orange circle on her cheeks. For special occasions she painted her entire body.

Comanche men wore breechcloths, leggings, and moccasins during the summer. During colder weather they added knee-high boots, and vests or shirts made from buffalo hide. Both men and women wore buffalo robes to protect themselves from the chilling winds of the open plains.

The men paid more attention to their hair than anything else. They allowed it to grow long, parting it in the middle with braids on each side of the part. The braids were wrapped with cloth or fur. Scalp locks, decorated with black or yellow feathers, hung from the top of their heads. Eyebrows and other facial hair were plucked out. Their ears were pierced in several places, allowing them to wear an assortment of decorative earrings. These were usually made from shells, or silver and brass rings.

SHELTER

The nomadic Comanche Indians lived in cone-shaped tepees. These easy to move dwellings were set up as close to wood and water as possible. The packing, setting up, taking down, and moving of the tepees was the responsibility of the women. By working together, several squaws could put up or take down a tepee in three to four minutes. To move the tepees the poles were placed into two equal bunches and tied with pieces of rawhide rope. The ropes were then strung through holes at the end of the poles and tied to each side of the horse. The upper ends of the poles rested on the horse's shoulders and the lower ends drug on the ground behind, thus forming a travois for easier travel.

A typical Comanche tepee was about thirteen feet high at the peak, but some, usually those of the chiefs, were as high as twenty-five feet. They used from sixteen to eighteen poles for the framework of the tepee. These were covered with buffalo skins that had been sewn together by the women of the tribe. Wooden pins and pegs were used to secure the skins to the ground. The door of the tepee was usually covered with bearskin.

In the center of the tepee a fire pit was made for

cooking and warmth. An opening at the top of the tepee allowed the smoke to escape. Along each side and at the back of the tepee were the beds, or seats. These were long platforms covered with reed mats and buffalo robes, or blankets.

The Comanches decorated the outside of their tepees with pictographs. These painted a picture of their life and usually included pictures of hunting, war parties, and brave deeds.

WEAPONS AND TOOLS

The Comanche Indians were experts with the bow and arrow. Their bows were made from Osage orange, ash, or hickory wood. They were strung with deer or buffalo sinew. Their arrows were made of dogwood that had been tipped with bone, flint, or steel. These were carried in a quiver case, which was strapped across the warrior's back.

The Comanche warrior was an excellent rider and fighter. He could hang over the side of his horse with only one foot across the horse's back and ride at full speed. This allowed the rider to be shielded from the enemy while he shot arrows underneath the neck of the horse. Most Comanches could shoot up to twenty arrows in one minute. His aim was usually right on target, and the speed of the arrows would sometimes send them all the way through the buffalo's body.

The Comanches were the first known North American Indians to use the lance and shield in battle. They learned how to use them to the best advantage from Coronado and his men in 1540. As the warriors lined up and prepared for battle, a chief or noted hero of the group rode out alone in front of the men. With only a lance in his hand he challenged the bravest of his enemy to combat.

They also used lances with sharpened bone points

for killing buffalo. They rode at full speed by the side of a buffalo. The lance was plunged into the heart of the animal, then jerked out immediately.

Shields were made of thick rawhide and shaped both round and oval. Thick rawhide taken from the neck of a buffalo, was stretched tightly over a frame and securely stitched. All shields were painted to represent the sun. The tribal symbol was painted inside the circle, along with rays of sun. The painting was done with red quicksilver ore called cinnabar. Feathers dangled from the rim of the shield to spoil the enemy's aim. Bear teeth attached to a warrior's shield showed that he was a mighty hunter, and scalps proved he was a brave warrior.

Before a shield was used in battle, it was highly regarded by its owner. However, after the battle was over it lost most of its importance and could be seen lying around the Comanche camps. Sometimes shields that had been used in battle were simply thrown away.

Later the Comanches acquired guns from the white man. A few revolvers were used as well as breech-loading rifles. Some of these were bought or traded for, and others were taken from the white settlers. When guns became more common among the tribes, shooting matches were held, with only the best marksman allowed to participate.

A long handled tool, called a battle axe, was used for cutting wood for the Comanche fires. With its extended handle and sharp edges, the battle axe was also carried into battle.

CUSTOMS AND RELIGION

The Comanches were a proud and independent people. They preferred to live by themselves and not mingle with other tribes. They wanted to keep a pure strain of Comanche blood.

Marriage was not permitted between anyone closer

than a second cousin. When a man found a girl he wished to marry, it was customary for him to give her father or brother a gift, which was usually a horse. Later, he sent an older relative to the girl's parents with more gifts. The relative offered the gifts to the family in exchange for the girl. If the family did not agree, the gifts were loaded on the back of the horse and the horse set free. If the family agreed to the proposal, the horses were added to the herd of the girl's family.

To the Comanches, the greatest age was the time spent as a warrior. A warrior was brave, aggressive, and sometimes cruel and vengeful. However, when a warrior became an older man of the tribe, he was expected to be thoughtful, considerate, and kind. This change was so difficult for some, they preferred to die while they were still young men.

When an older person approached death, his family sometimes abandoned him. It was not that they no longer loved him, but that they feared evil spirits associated with death. When an older man knew he was dying, he gave away his personal property and went to a lonely spot to die. After death, burial took place immediately. The body was bathed, the eyes sealed with clay, and the face painted red. He was dressed in his finest for burial.

If the earth was soft, making digging with a spade made of buffalo bone easy, the Comanches buried their dead standing straight up, with their face toward the rising sun. However, the earth was usually so hard it was difficult to dig deep enough to keep the body safe from wolves and other animals. Therefore, most of the time the knees were drawn up to the chest, the head bent forward, and the body tied in this position. A blanket was tied around the body and placed on a horse. Women, weeping and wailing, rode on either side of the body as it was taken to the final resting place. The body was then wedged into the grave in a sitting position or on its side, facing the rising sun.

The Comanches sometimes used the scaffold for burial. Scaffolds were made of poles and the bodies were placed on top of them.

When a young warrior died, the mourning period lasted for a long time. Comanche women cut gashes in their faces, arms, and legs with broken glass or knives. If the warrior was a close relative, they might also cut off a finger. Sometimes the men cut their hair and cut gashes in their bodies during the mourning period. They also spent hours smoking and praying. Personal items, such as knives, bows and lances, were buried with a warrior. His favorite horse was often shot at the grave.

The Comanches, unlike some of the other Indian tribes, were not afraid of the dead. Nevertheless, they avoided using names of the dead, and if a chief or some other important person of the tribe died, the entire tribe moved. This was done so relatives of the dead were not reminded of their loved one.

Each family group had a peace chief. He was usually one of the older men. Even though the Comanches listened to his advice, the peace chief did not have much power. Important matters of the tribe, such as moving, religious ceremonies, and buffalo hunts, were decided by the tribal council. The war chiefs were chosen for their bravery in battle. They led the warriors on raiding parties as well as in battle, and made decisions on when to retreat and when to continue fighting.

The Comanche Indians seemed to mix ceremony, medicine, and religion. Medicine men carried a small basket or bag containing what they called their "spirits." Inside the container were a variety of roots, hair from a deer, owl heads, animal teeth, and even small pebbles. He tried to heal the sick by counting and rattling a long string of beads he wore around his neck.

The medicine man was best at healing snake bites.

Immediately after a victim had been bitten a fire was built, and the tip of the medicine man's arrow was heated. With the arrow, he bored into the holes made by the snake and destroyed the poison before it had time to absorb into the bloodstream.

Supernatural powers were given to men through visions. Those who had great powers believed they could pass it on to others. Women received power through their husbands.

The Comanches were not afraid of the dead or ghosts. On a war party a ghost might appear to a warrior in the form of a skeleton.

They thought the sun, moon, and earth were supernatural beings, and they believed in a greater power called Our Sure Enough Father, or The Great Spirit. They also believed in an Evil Spirit.

One of the most feared supernatural powers was thunder. The Comanches believed it appeared as a mighty bird, even more powerful than an Eagle. This thunderbird brought thunder, rain, and storms to the people.

Animals were also a source of power. They believed that the buffalo could talk to the people, eagles knew about war, a bear could cure wounds, and the elk was filled with strength. The coyote was their brother.

Smoking was a part of Comanche ceremonies. Their pipes were made from a long dogwood stem about the size of a pencil, which measured up to thirty inches long and feathered at the end. The ceremonial peace pipe was made from the red clay of South Dakota. It was always kept by the chief or medicine man.

The Comanches believed in life after death. They believed it would be a happy life, filled with plenty of buffalo, peace, and everlasting youth.

CHILDREN

As soon as a baby was born it was bathed, wrapped in soft skins, and placed on a cradleboard. Both boys and girls were welcomed into the family, but there was greater joy when a boy was born. They believed that since a boy would become a warrior and the protector of the people, he was superior to a girl.

Pet names were given to the children until they could be formally named. An important person in the tribe was usually asked to name the baby. Then, in a formal ceremony, the shaman puffed smoke to the heavens, held the baby up, and offered a prayer.

A Comanche baby's movement was very limited. Until he was nine or ten months old, he was kept on the cradleboard during the day. At night he slept between his parents.

Young Comanche boys wore no clothes at all when the weather was warm. Later they wore a breechcloth, leggings, and moccasins. The girls always wore some kind of clothing even in warm weather. When it was cold they wore buffalo robes, knee-high boots, leggings, and moccasins.

Children learned the ways of the Comanches by observing their parents and others in the tribe. Girls were given tasks by their mothers, and the boys learned to hunt and ride with their fathers. Parents reasoned with their children and never gave whippings as a means of punishment.

A young girl was sometimes given a feast. During the celebration she would run behind a fast pony, hanging on to its tail as she ran. This proved that she was able to move quickly and easily.

As boys became older, they tended to avoid girls and stay together in groups. Before a boy was allowed to go on a raid or with a war party, he had to receive supernatural powers through a vision. After he was successful on the warpath, a dance, called the Giveway Dance, was arranged by his father. During this dance, the family gave away all their belongings, to show the tribe they believed their son would obtain new wealth for them. This marked the beginning of manhood and gave the new warrior the right to marry.

CYNTHIA ANN PARKER

Cynthia Ann Parker, the daughter of early Texas settlers, played an important role in the history of the Comanche Indians.

John Parker, his family and a large number of relatives, built a fort near present-day Groesbeck, Texas. Parker's Fort was built on a small hill overlooking the Navasota River.

The land was fertile so crops were planted, cared for, and harvested by the pioneers. During the day, all able-bodied members of the fort went to the fields to work until late in the evening. Women, older men, and children were left at the fort. They felt safe within the thick walls of the fort. When the workers returned from the fields, the large gate was closed and locked for the night.

On a warm, sunny day in 1836, the men left the fort to work in the fields, carelessly leaving the gate unlocked. Later in the morning one of the younger children, playing at the entrance to the fort, began to scream. He had seen about five hundred mounted Comanche Indians in the distance. Everyone inside the fort came running. They were offered a ray of hope when they noticed that the warriors were carrying a white flag, which meant they came in peace.

Benjamin, a member of the Parker family, went out to talk to the Indians. He reported to the group that the Indians were seeking food and directions to a nearby waterhole. He then returned to the Indians and continued talking, hoping to prevent an attack. However, when he approached the Indians once more, they attacked and killed Benjamin. Then, the warriors rode into the fort, screaming, shouting, and killing the settlers. Nine-year-old Cynthia Ann Parker and her little brother John were captured by the Comanches and taken to their camp.

Cynthia Ann Parker was raised as an Indian. She dressed like the Comanches, followed their laws and customs, and spoke their language. She was given the Comanche name, Naduah. When she was about sixteen years of age, Cynthia Ann married Peta Nocona, a Comanche chief. They had several children, and her son Quanah Parker was the last war chief of the Comanches.

During her early years of captivity, Texas settlers searched for Cynthia Ann and her brother. She went unrecognized for a long period of time since she looked exactly like an Indian.

In December of 1860, Texas Rangers attacked a Comanche band, and Peta Nocona was killed in the battle. Cynthia Ann and her daughter, Prairie Flower, tried to escape, but one of the men noticed her blue eyes and knew she was not an Indian. They took her to her uncle, Isaac Parker, who lived near Fort Worth. She begged to return to the Indians and the only life she had ever known. But the Rangers sent her to other members of the Parker family in East Texas.

Cynthia Ann Parker never learned to adapt to the white man's ways. She continued to grieve for her husband and sons, and a few years after being taken back to the white man's world, her daughter, Prairie Flower, died. Shortly after, Cynthia Ann also died.

QUANAH PARKER

Quanah Parker, the son of Comanche Chief Peta Nocona, was born in 1845. His mother was Cynthia Ann Parker, a white woman who had been captured by the Comanches when she was only a child of nine.

Because he was half-white and half-Indian, Quanah was sometimes mistreated by members of his own tribe. Therefore, at a very young age he leaned to defend himself and became a strong warrior.

In December of 1860, Texas Rangers and cavalrymen attacked Peta Nocona's Comanche camp. Quanah and his father were on a buffalo hunt that day, and when they returned they found the camp in ruins. The tepees had been burned and many Comanches had been killed. Those that escaped were moaning and wailing in grief. Quanah's mother and baby sister, Prairie Flower, were not there. The Rangers had recognized Cynthia Ann and returned her to the Parker family.

When his father died from an infected wound, Quanah left his father's band and joined the Kwahadis, who lived in the Texas Panhandle. They were the most hostile Comanche band. Even though other Indian tribes were signing peace treaties with the United States government and agreeing to live on reservations, the Kwahadis refused.

Later, white buffalo hunters joined the United States Cavalry in their fight against the Indians. When the buffalo hunters moved south into the Texas Panhandle, the army officials did not try to stop them. They believed if the Indians no longer had buffalo to supply their food, clothing, and shelter, they would have no trouble putting them on reservations and keeping them there.

The Indians were angered by the needless slaughter of the buffalo. They knew that without the buffalo their way of life would be doomed. Comanches, Kiowas, Cheyennes, and Arapahos met at a war council. Quanah

Parker was chosen to lead a raid on the buffalo hunters at Adobe Walls in the Texas Panhandle. Even though the Indian bands were defeated in this battle, they continued to fight the army and the buffalo hunters for another year.

Finally, Quanah Parker led his people to Fort Sill, Oklahoma, where they surrendered to the U.S. Army. This ragged group of Comanche Indians were the last to live freely on the Texas Plains and the last to surrender their freedom to the white man.

Quanah Parker knew he must forget the past and live in peace. He owned cattle, horses, and land. He helped build schools, and he taught the Indians how to plant and harvest crops. He made many trips to Washington on behalf of his people. The town of Quanah, Texas, was named after him. Parker County was named for his mother, and the town of Nocona was named for his father.

Quanah Parker died on February 23, 1911. He is buried beside his mother at Fort Sill, Oklahoma. His large red granite tombstone reads:

> Resting here until day breaks,
> and shadows fall,
> and darkness disappears, is
> QUANAH PARKER
> LAST CHIEF OF THE COMANCHES.

IRON SHIRT

In the 1850s, a Comache chief named Iron Shirt, led a band of Comanches through the northern and central plains of Texas. Since there were many settlements in the central part of the state, this became a favorite target for surprise attacks and raids.

It was believed by some people that Iron Shirt had supernatural powers. Many who had tried to kill the chief were unable to do so. Even though Iron Shirt was shot many times, he was never harmed. Later, it was learned the secret of staying alive was in the shirt he wore. It was made of iron. The shirt, which once belonged to a Spanish conquistador, had been handed down from his ancestors.

The Texas Rangers were anxious to put an end to the Comanche raids, and in April of 1858, over one hundred rangers rode toward the Comanche camp. One hundred and thirteen Tonkawa Indians, who were friendly to the white man, joined the Rangers.

After they crossed the Red River, scouts spotted the Comanche warriors. The Rangers hid their wagons and rode toward the camp. When they were close enough for battle, John S. Ford, leader of the Rangers, ordered an attack. Led by the Tonkawas, the Rangers rode into the Comanche camp. Iron Shirt had been warned by two of his warriors and was ready for battle. He rode his grey mount back and forth in front of the Rangers, daring them to shoot. The Ranger's bullets ricocheted from his armor, and he continued to ride before the enemy yelling blood-curdling war cries.

When Iron Shirt turned to go back to his warriors, one of the Rangers took aim and fired. Iron Shirt fell to the ground. When his warriors saw their fallen leader, they became frightened and fled north. The Ranger's carefully aimed bullet had been fired underneath the plate of armor, ending Iron Shirt's life.

CONCLUSION

For three centuries the plains had been the home of the Comanche Indians. They were free to set up camps and move freely in this land they called theirs. They were magnificent horsemen and hunters. By following the buffalo herds they were able to provide their people with the necessary food, clothing, and shelter.

With the coming of the white settlers and the

strength of the Texas Rangers, the Comanche way of life was in great danger. The buffalo became more and more scarce, as buffalo hunters moved into their territory. Between 1830 and 1860, it became more difficult for the Comanches to feed their families through hunting alone. Therefore, they began raids on the white settlers — taking their food, horses, and sometimes their lives.

Even though the Comanches were greatly feared by the white settlers, it is easy to see why they fought so hard and long. General Philip Sheridan, a member of the United States Army who encouraged the killing of the buffalo, probably said it better than anyone else: "We took away their country and means of support. We broke up their mode of living, their habits of life, introduced disease and decay among them. And it was for this and against this that they made war. Could anyone expect less?"

The Comanches, like other Indian tribes, were a defeated people. In 1900, they signed a treaty with the United States giving the federal government control of the tribe. The chiefs and warriors marched single file into the "Big Smoke Talk" council. Wearing full Indian regalia, including war bonnets, they stood with their heads held high. The proud Comanches stood strong and tall to the end.

The United States government then placed the Comanches, along with other Indian tribes, on reservations.

The Apaches

The Apache (ah-PAH-chee) Indians lived in small family groups and called themselves Tinde, which meant "the people."

The Apaches lived in the northern part of Texas until they were forced off their land by the Comanches. The Lipan Apaches lived in an area which extended west from the Texas Hill Country to the Rio Grande. The Mescalero Apaches lived in New Mexico, from the Rio Grande in the west, to the Pecos River in Texas near the town of Pecos.

Other Apache groups lived in Arizona, New Mexico, Mexico, Kansas, Oklahoma, and Colorado. Territory was staked out by each Apache group. They stayed within family groups as they hunted buffalo and cared for their people. However, during wartime the family groups joined together and were united into bands.

FOOD

The Apaches were hunters, and meat was a large part of their diet. They hunted buffalo, deer, antelope, rabbits, and even rodents.

They prepared the buffalo meat in a variety of ways. It was baked, boiled, roasted, and sometimes eaten raw. Some of the meat was dried on racks and made into jerky. The blood of the buffalo was used to thicken soups, stews, and puddings.

Deer hunting was done all year long and provided much of their meat supply. The day before a deer hunt Apaches would not eat strong-smelling foods for fear the deer could detect it. To prevent the deer from smelling the Apache's own body odor they smeared their bodies with animal fat.

Several hunters would leave the camp together, but once they arrived at the hunting ground they worked alone or in pairs. In order to get to their prey, they sometimes wore a deer mask made from the stuffed head of a deer and fitted on their shoulders. A skillful hunter would be able to get within a few feet of the deer without causing any alarm.

After the kill, the deer had to be skinned and butchered properly. Its head was laid toward the east, and the hunter never walked around the front of it, nor did he step over it. He severed the tendons of the lower legs to keep the legs limp, making it easier for him to work.

If the hunter did not have a horse, he carried as much of the deer back to camp with him as possible. The rest of the deer was strung in a tree until he was able to return. He carried the hooves and head with him as a sign of good luck.

Deer meat was usually boiled or fried when it was fresh. Sometimes it was made into a stew, and dumplings were made to be eaten with it. Like the buffalo, it was also made into jerky to be eaten later in the year.

Apache women gathered vegetables, fruits, nuts, and roots. They found strawberries, mulberries, walnuts, piñon nuts, and sunflower seeds.

Two of the most important wild plants eaten by the Lipan Apaches were the agave and sotol plants. The tender leaves of the sotol plant were roasted in hot coals before they were eaten. To prepare the bulb of the plant for eating, rocks were put into a roaring fire, and kept there until there were very hot. Then the ashes were removed and the bulbs placed on the rocks. The rocks and bulbs were covered with dirt. Several days later the bulbs were removed and cooked. When they were done they were raked out and left to cool. Then the Apache women beat the bulbs into thin sheets and let them dry in the sun. The sotol could then be eaten as it was, or it could be ground into flour and made into ashcakes.

The piñon pine nut was another source of plant food for the Apaches. The cones were dried and roasted and then .the nuts were removed. They could be eaten as they were, or they could be mixed with other foods. Sometimes they were ground into flour and made into thick bread or boiled in soups.

When the women searched for food, they also looked for beehives hidden in the stalks of cactus plants. They smoked the bees from the hive, used a stone to break the hive, and took the honey. Honey was a rare and welcomed treat for them.

There were some foods the Apaches would never eat. Snakes, prairie dogs, fish, and turkeys were believed to be unclean. Mountain lions were sometimes eaten, but they were not a desirable food for the Apaches. They rarely ate birds of any kind, but when they did they were usually boiled.

CLOTHING

The women prepared the animal skins and made all the clothing for her family. The rawhide that was used for making a tepee was too coarse and rough to be made into clothing. Many hours of preparation took place before any clothing could be made from buffalo skin.

First, the hide was scraped clean with a tool that had been made from a buffalo bone. Then it was tied to a frame made of poles to be tanned. This tanning process was accomplished by rubbing a mixture of buffalo liver, fat, and brains into the hide to make it softer and more pliable. Then the skin was soaked in water, wrung out, and put back on the frame. Later it would be pulled, stretched, and rubbed until it was smooth and soft all over. From these soft skins, the Apaches made shirts, skirts, and leggings. Winter robes were made from skins that had only been tanned on one side. The hair was worn on the inside to make the robe much warmer.

During the warm summer months, Apache men wore a breechcloth, leggings, and moccasins. When the weather grew colder, they added a blanket and buckskin shirt. They did not want to be restrained in any way, whether in battle or on a buffalo hunt. Therefore, they wore loose-fitting, round-necked shirts or tunics. They usually sewed fringes into the sleeves with deer sinew and added beadwork to the shirt as well. Sometimes when the weather was extremely cold the men wore loose fitting jackets made of deer or elk skins. These were made with no sleeves, similar to a poncho.

Apache warriors cut their hair on the left side even with the top of their ear. They let the right side of their hair grow long, and it sometimes reached the ground. They pulled their long hair into a loop, tied it with deer sinew, and decorated it with feathers and trinkets. They pierced from six to eight holes in the left ear and one or more in the right ear. For special occasions ornaments were worn in each of these holes.

They wanted no hair on their face at all, and spent much of their spare time plucking out their eyebrows and beard. Their faces and bodies were smeared with several colors of paint.

Apache women wore leggings, moccasins, fringed and beaded dresses, or a buckskin skirt and top. A sharp bone knife was used to cut out the dress, and it was stitched together with sinew. Usually the skirt was made from two tanned elk skins hung over a belt, one in front and one in back. The bottom of the skirt was cut in deep fringe. Over her dress she sometimes wore a short cape and tied a belt around her waist. These were decorated with porcupine quills, elk teeth, and beads.

Moccasins, worn by both men and women, came up to the knee. The fold at the knee served as pockets. The soles of the moccasins were made from undressed hides and tended to turn up at the toes. During the winter, the moccasins were stuffed with grass or hair for additional warmth.

An Apache woman wore her hair long with one thick braid hanging down her back. For special occasions she would allow her hair to flow freely down her shoulders and back. Earrings made of beads and copper wire were favorite means of decoration. Polished copper rings were worn at the wrists and ankles, and necklaces were made from clam shells.

A headdress was very important to an Apache warrior. A feathered headdress was only worn for special occasions, which included war dances and council meetings. Apache warbonnets were made of eagle feathers. Each feather represented a brave deed, and a warbonnet made of eagle feathers was highly valued. If a warrior had a warbonnet made from one perfect tail of twelve feathers and the feathers were white with black tips, the bonnet was worth one pony.

SHELTER

Since the Apaches were primarily buffalo hunters and constantly on the move, their dwellings had to be easy to move. Apache tribes living further west in Arizona and New Mexico lived in wickiups. A wickiup was a circular or oval dwelling made of brush. The floors were dirt that had been scooped out to make the living area larger. In summer leafy branches were draped over the dwelling, and in the winter they added animal skins for additional warmth.

In Texas, however, the tepee provided shelter for the Apaches. They used light poles, usually sotol stalks, to form the framework for the tepee. The heavy ends of the stalks were placed in the circle, and the lighter part of the stalk was tied together at the top. The poles were often as high as twenty-five feet. Fifteen to eighteen buffalo skins were sewn together and thrown over the poles, leaving an opening at the top for a smoke hole. These skins were held down by wooden pegs. The door to the tepee was a flap of skin stretched over a frame. These entrances always faced toward the east.

Beside the tepee was a large brush arbor. This was a cooler place for the Apaches to eat and rest.

Inside the tepee were beds or seats. One was placed in the back of the tepee and the other two were on each side of the wall. They were long platforms covered with mats of light willow rods. Buffalo blankets, or robes, covered the willow rods. The Apaches used pictographs to decorate the inside and outside of their homes. These picture stories illustrated Apache life, and scenes of hunting and war were usually chosen.

The women of the tribe were responsible for the tepees. They tanned the hides, sewed them together with sinew, and set them up. When several women worked together, a tepee could be erected in three minutes. When it was time for the tribe to move, it was the job of the women to take down the tepee, pack it on a travois, and see that it arrived safely at the next camp.

WEAPONS AND TOOLS

The bow and arrow were the principal weapons of the Apache Indians. A warrior spent much of his time making arrows, and when he went on a raid he had about forty arrows in his quiver. The arrows were made of hard wood with the bark scraped smooth. By working the bark against a heated rock the arrow could be made much straighter. The ends were whittled to a fine point and tipped with iron points. Each arrow was decorated with bands of different colored paints so a warrior could recognize his own arrow.

Apache bows were about four feet long, and the best ones were made from Mulberry wood. The branch was stripped of its bark, split, and shaped into a bow. It was left several days to dry. Then it was pulled and rubbed until it could be bent into shape. The bow was tied securely and placed in hot ashes so it would keep its shape.

Bowstrings were usually made from deer sinew that had been soaked in water. The sinew was peeled into strands, spliced end to end, and made into one long bowstring. A warrior usually carried extra bowstrings with him in case the one he was using snapped.

Quivers were made of calf or deerskin and were usually about four feet long. However, it was considered good luck if one could be made of mountain lion skins. Quivers were carried over the warrior's back, but during battle they were put under the left armpit for easier reach.

Lances made from the sotol stalk or some other light material, usually averaged seven to eight feet long. These were sometimes decorated with blue and red paint with one or two eagle feathers fastened to the base of the point. They had steel blades fastened to wooden poles and held in place by a cow's tail slipped over one end. Lances were used in close battle. A warrior who used the lance was very brave because he had to spear the enemy at close range.

War clubs were also used by the Apaches. A round rock, about the size of the warrior's fist, was put inside a rawhide pouch. This was attached to a wooden handle by a piece of rawhide that had been twisted to make the club stronger. The handle was covered with buckskin, and a loop was sewn to the end for the warrior's hand.

Knives were used by the Apache Indians in battle and during a buffalo hunt. They were made of flint and very crudely done. Some were carried underneath the belt, and others were put in plain buckskin sheaths.

Guns that had been stolen or traded for were sometimes used. However, since the early rifles had to be loaded each time they were shot, the Apache found he could shoot a dozen or more arrows in the time it took him to load the rifle. Also, when the warrior was riding at full speed, the rifle was much less accurate than the bow and arrow.

All Apache tools were made of natural materials. Tools for digging were usually made from buffalo bones, wood, or antlers. Scraping tools were made from stone.

CUSTOMS AND RELIGION

The Apache god was called Ysun, which meant the giver of life. They believed that Ysun sent spirits and powers to teach them how to live.

The Apaches believed that everything in the universe was given power. This power could be good, such as giving life and health to the people. It could be bad when it brought illness and death. The power could also be used to make the enemies week and protect the Apaches from attacks. It allowed the shaman to diagnose and cure any illness they might have.

Some healing ceremonies involved pollen, as it represented health. The ceremony began with the patient and all his relatives and other members of the group attending. The patient showed his respect for the shaman by calling his name. Then he traced a cross on the shaman's right foot with the pollen. Other parts of the shaman's body were sprinkled with the pollen, and another cross was drawn on his left foot. When this was finished, the shaman began his work. He rolled a cigarette, and blew smoke north, south, east, and west. These cardinal directions were thought to be sacred. After the shaman called upon his power for healing of the patient, he and the sick person marked each other with pollen. The shaman sang and prayed that the illness might be cured.

This ceremony was repeated on four consecutive nights, starting when it became dark and ending at midnight. After midnight, everyone ate food that had been prepared by the patient's family. At the end of the ceremony the shaman sucked out poison that had been planted into the patient by an evil power and spit the poison into the fire. He sometimes gave the patient a charm that would protect him from future illness.

The Apaches believed there was also power in death. When someone died, their relatives began a time of mourning. They put on old clothing, cut their hair, and began to cry and wail. Most of the Apaches were afraid of the dead and would not touch the dead bodies. Sometimes they asked strangers, or forced captives to prepare the body for burial. Some groups used a horse in their burial ceremony. The body was placed on the horse along with his possessions and led away from camp. The body was hidden in crevices of rocks. Some of his belongings were placed in the crevice with him and the rest of his belongings were destroyed. Then the horse was killed and the burial party returned to camp, where they burned the clothing they were wearing and cleansed themselves.

Because they were afraid of the spirits of the dead returning to them, they never spoke the name of the dead person again. The name was never given to another person so the dead person's name also died with him.

They believed owls and bears were a form of ghosts sent to hurt their people. An owl feather was thought to bring illness or death.

The Apaches did not have a formal place for worship, but their religion was a part of their everyday life. The Apache leader, Geronimo, explained the religious attitude of his people in his book *Geronimo's Story of His Life* in this manner.

> We had no churches, no religious organizations no Sabbath day, no holidays, and yet we worshipped. Sometimes the whole tribe would assemble to sing and pray; sometimes in a smaller number, perhaps only two or three . . . Sometimes we prayed in silence; sometimes each one prayed aloud; sometimes an aged person prayed for all of us.

Marriage was a very important event in the lives of the Apaches. When a boy and girl were married, they went to live with the girl's family, which included her parents, grandparents, cousins, aunts, neices, and unmarried uncles and nephews. The mother-in-law was an important person in the family group. For example, when her son-in-law brought fresh game to the camp, she cooked the meat and divided it among other members of the group.

Ceremonies were held before a war party left the camp. The night before a raid the older squaws would go some distance from the camp. There they spent the night, singing a strange and mournful chant. The next morning the war party would leave the camp.

If the war party had been successful, the warriors sang as they came near the camp so all the people could come out to greet them. When they arrived in camp, they sat in a circle and slapped their thighs in time with the music. Later, a victory dance was performed which included a scalp dance. The old squaws once again began their night of chants.

Storytelling was a favorite custom of the Apache people. It provided an opportunity for the people to get together to share their stories and myths. These story-telling sessions were usually announced to the group so everyone could come. Sometimes the stories continued through the night, and a meal was served to the people by the storyteller.

The Apaches believed the number four was a lucky number. Sometimes they would do things four times in order to have good luck. The four cardinal directions (north, south, east, and west) were very important to them.

When there was a murder within the group, the punishment for the murderer was decided on by the family of the victim. First, the murderer was taken to the killer's family, and if he had been a constant trouble-maker they might kill him themselves. If not, they could help him to escape until a money settlement could be made with the victim's family. Sometimes, if they believed him to be innocent, they could side with the murderer and a long feud among the families would begin.

If someone in the camp continued to commit crimes, he was banished from the group. Word spread quickly, and nearby camps would not allow him to stay there either. So, the criminal found himself hiding in the wilderness, not accepted by anyone.

CHILDREN

Children were prized members of the Apache Indians. The Lipan Apaches believed that when a child was born, a small whirlwind entered into the child's body through the throat and kept it warm. Immediately after birth the child was held up to all four directions as well as to the sun. About four days later the child was given a name by its father and placed on a cradleboard.

Babies were taught at a very early age the importance of being quiet. If a baby cried to get attention, it might be taken to a bush closeby and left until the crying stopped. The Apaches realized that a crying baby might give away their location to the enemy.

When the child was six to eight months old it was allowed to leave the cradleboard and move freely about the camp. Sometime during his first year an Apache boy was given his first haircut. The child's hair was cut short, leaving only a few strands of long hair. His hair was cut three more times and then it was never cut again.

When children were old enough they were expected to help with the chores of the family. They learned to dress themselves, gather firewood, and work with adults within the family group.

As the children went about their chores and daily life, they were also taught about their culture. The adults told them stories about their history, behavior that was expected of them, religion, and fables. Sometimes the stories were about real people and events, and other times they were stories that had been handed down through their families and were not necessarily true.

As Apache boys grew older, they were encouraged to become strong, brave warriors. One way of accomplishing this was to be exposed to many hardships, such as exposing their bodies for long periods of time to the sun. They were told stories of hunting and great war parties. They learned to hunt and make their own weapons. They practiced running long distances to give them endurance. On their first hunting and raiding trips they were not allowed to hunt or fight. They did other chores within the camp, such as gathering wood, cooking, and tending the horses. Usually, by their late teens they became warriors and were given full Apache privileges.

Apache children were rarely ever spanked. If a child was really unruly, he might be doused with water.

Apache girls worked with their mothers and other members of the family group. They learned to cook, clean the animal hides, put up a tepee, and care for the younger children.

When an Apache girl and boy were ready for marriage, the boy had to ask permission from the girl's father or some other male relative. If the girl's parents agreed to the marriage, the bridegroom brought the family gifts of horses, skins, and guns. For the marriage ceremony heated rocks were placed on the side of a large beef hide so that it curled up into a rough container. The container was taken to a secluded place, and water was poured into it. When the bride and groom arrived, they held hands and walked around in the water. Then everyone walked back to the village. A dance was held in celebration of the marriage.

VICTORIO

Victorio was chief of the Chiricahua Apaches and was considered to be a skilled leader. Some even thought he was feared more than the Apache Chief Geronimo.

Victorio knew the Trans-Pecos area of Texas well. He knew the best places for camping, and where game could be found.

However, United States troops and Texas Rangers were sent to drive Victorio and his men into Mexico. They were chased into the Candelaria Mountains, where they raided small settlements and stole horses and food.

The Texans knew that as long as Victorio and his men were allowed to raid settlements in Mexico it would be easy for them to cross to our side of the Rio Grande once more. Even though the Rangers joined the Mexicans in trying to stop Victorio and his men, they were able to escape and continued raiding for another year.

In 1880, a message was sent to the United States that Victorio was thought to be heading for the Eagle

Mountains in Texas. Again, the Mexican army and the Texas Rangers tried to capture the cunning leader. Again, they failed.

On October 14, 1880, a Mexican general and his cavalry found Victorio and his men in the mountains of Chihuahua and attacked. Victorio, his sixty warriors, and eighteen women were all killed. Other squaws and children were taken prisoners.

During his final battle, Victorio mounted a white horse and rode out in full view of the cavalry. He was shot with two bullets at long range.

During his lifetime, Victorio fought in more than two hundred skirmishes or battles. Many soldiers agreed that he was a military genius. Some believed Victorio was our greatest American Indian chief.

FLACCO

Flacco was not only loved by his people, but he was also a friend of the white man. He was a friend and comrade of Captain Jack Hays of the United States Army and fought with him in many battles against the Comanches.

Once in a battle with the Comanches, Captain Hays was on a runaway horse that ran straight toward the enemy. Flacco thought this was a planned action and so he followed Hays. The Comanches were so surprised by this action they could only sit on their horses and watch.

Chief Flacco was described by James K. Greer in his biography of Jack Hays, as being tall and strong, and always well-dressed. He wore wrist bands and armlets of pure silver and a string of beads around his neck. He carried his quiver in a wide belt he wore across his chest. Inside the belt at his waist was a hunting knife. White buckskin leggings came to his knees and were decorated with wide fringe and figures painted in black and red. His moccasins were also fringed and decorated with beads.

When the Mexicans invaded San Antonio in 1842, Flacco became a scout to lead an invasion into Mexico. Another Lipan Apache, who was a deaf-mute, also accompanied him. On their way back from a raid the deaf-mute became ill in San Antonio, and they stopped. Later, two white men were seen in Seguin with Flacco's horses, and Flacco and the deaf-mute were dead.

However, Flacco's father was told that he had been killed by Mexicans, for fear the Apaches would take vengence on the white settlers.

Flacco had given many years of faithful service to the white man, and all who knew him respected him. Sam Houston, president of the Republic of Texas, sent shawls to the young chief's wives and a message of sympathy to his father.

GERONIMO

The Chiricahua Apaches, led by Geronimo, were ordered to go to the San Carlos Reservation in New Mexico. Unhappy with their life on the reservation, Geronimo and his followers managed to escape. They traveled through West Texas, raiding settlers along the way before crossing the border into Mexico.

Since the Apaches hated the Mexicans so much, Geronimo had no difficulty gaining more followers. Large herds of cattle and horses were stolen and sold to settlers in New Mexico. With the money, the Apaches bought clothes, guns, and ammunition.

General George Crook, a famous Indian fighter, was put in charge of capturing Geronimo and his men. Crook wanted to be fair with the Apaches, and he made plans to meet with Geronimo. The opportunity came when Geronimo and his men left the camp on a raiding party. By the time Geronimo returned, Crook and his soldiers had taken control of the camp. Geronimo and Crook held three long meetings before coming to terms.

Crook promised the Apaches they would be treated fairly if they returned to the reservation, and he gave Geronimo all the time he needed to gather his men and return to San Carlos.

Eight months later Geronimo and his followers surrendered, and for more than a year the Apaches stayed on the reservation. However, after a night of drinking, Geronimo and one hundred and thirty four of his followers escaped from the reservation. It was almost ten months before they were recaptured.

President Grover Cleveland wanted Geronimo hung. He was sent to a Florida prison instead and later to Fort Sill, Oklahoma, where he died in 1909. Geronimo was never allowed to return to his Apache homeland.

CONCLUSION

By the middle of the early 1700s, several groups of Apache Indians had entered Texas, making their home on the open plains. They were content with their way of life, hunting the buffalo and tending to their daily needs.

Life was not easy for these nomadic Indians. Most of their years in Texas were spent at war. They became bitter enemies of the Comanches who pushed them off their hunting grounds in Central Texas. Threatened by white settlers as well, the Apaches could do nothing less than fight for their heritage and their land.

Perhaps Geronimo, the feared Apache leader, said it best in his autobiography.

> We are vanishing from the earth, yet I cannot think we are useless or Usen [God] would not have created us. . . .
>
> Usen created the Apaches, He also created their homes in the West. He gave them such grain, fruits, and game as they needed to eat. To restore their health when disease attacked them He taught them where to find these herbs, and how to prepare them

for medicine. He gave them a pleasant climate, and all they needed for clothing and shelter was at hand. Thus it was in the beginning: the Apaches and their homes each created for the other by Usen Himself. When they are taken from these homes they sicken and die. How long will it be until it is said there are no Apaches?

The Alabama-Coushattas

The Alabama-Coushatta (koo-SHOT-tah) Indians are two separate tribes, but because they have been so closely related throughout history, they have come to be recognized as one.

The Alabamas and Coushattas once lived in the present state of Alabama, near what is now known as the city of Montgomery. They also lived in parts of Mississippi and Georgia. The name Alabama means "vegetation gatherers," and Coushatta refers to "cane, reed, or white cane."

The first explorer to meet the Alabama-Coushatta Indians was Hernado de Soto, in 1541. Very little was known about the tribes until they came in contact with the French in the early 1700s.

In 1763, the Alabama and Coushatta tribes left their homes in Alabama and migrated to southern Louisiana. Some settled along the Red River, but the majority of both tribes built villages along the Sabine River.

By 1780, the Alabamas and the Coushattas had begun crossing the border into East Texas. Both tribes were welcomed by the Spanish officials. The Alabamas built their villages along the Neches River, while the Coushattas settled along the Trinity River. Since these rivers were within forty miles of each other, and the language of the Alabamas and the Coushattas was similar, visits between the two tribes were not uncommon.

103

In the days before the Texas Revolution, Sam Houston sent representatives to speak to the leaders of the Alabama-Coushattas. He wanted to be sure of their friendship. Later, Sam Houston himself visited the Alabama-Coushatta villages. He advised them to stay out of the fighting, stating, "It is not your war." He promised to keep them posted and advise them of their safety during the war. Sam Houston believed if the Indians remained neutral during the Texas Revolution the winner of the war could have no grudge against the "redman."

Some of the Alabamas chose to return to Louisiana until the war was over. However, the Coushattas stayed and helped the Texans by feeding those settlers who were fleeing Santa Anna's soldiers.

After Texas won its independence from Mexico, more and more white settlers began moving into the Alabama-Coushatta's homeland. When Mirabeau B. Lamar became president of the Republic of Texas, he suggested the tribe move to a location on the Brazos River. When the chiefs saw the site that had been chosen for them, they did not want to go. Then it was suggested they might be moved to the "Indian Territory," in what is now the state of Oklahoma.

In 1840, a petition was made to grant the Alabama-Coushattas two pieces of land between the Neches and Trinity rivers. This land included the villages already established by the tribes. However, the tribes did not know how to register their land at the land office and white settlers continued to push their way onto the land.

When Texas became a part of the United States, General Sam Houston heard the Indians were having difficulty keeping their lands. He told the tribes they should ask the new government for help. Thus, with the help of Sam Houston, the Alabama-Coushatta Indians were awarded 1,280 acres of land on Big Sandy Creek for a reservation. Title to the land was given to the Alabamas, tax free.

In 1855, the Texas Legislature approved 640 acres of land for the Coushattas. However, the land was not suitable for crops, and hunting in the Big Thicket was not what it had once been. Living conditions on the reservation were not good. There was hunger and even starvation among the people, and the housing conditions were poor. Many went to work in logging camps or on the farms of the white settlers in order to survive. In 1910, it was noted that there were only two hundred and two Alabama-Coushatta Indians living in Texas, compared to more than a thousand less than a hundred years before.

When the federal government saw the plight of the Alabama-Coushattas, it bought an additional 3,071 acres of land next to the original reservation. The government also provided better housing, as well as educational and medical help.

FOOD

Even though the soil was sandy and not very good for raising crops, the Alabama-Coushattas did raise some food from their gardens. They grew beans, corn, squash, melons, and pumpkins. They also had orchards, which produced fresh fruit for the tribe. In addition to fruits and vegetables they added water lily buds, butterfly weed, and duck potato tubers to their diet.

Their most important crop was corn. After the harvest, the corn was dried and ground into meal. Most cultures used stones for grinding corn, but the Alabama-Coushattas used wood because it was so plentiful in the Big Thicket. The mortar, a strong wooden bowl used for pounding the corn, was made from a log with part of the center hollowed out. A long, wooden pole was used to pound the corn into meal.

Sometimes the meal was poured into a pot of boiling water to make a cornmeal mush called bobsey, or it was added to other ingredients to make a soup called sofkey. The finely ground meal was used for making bread and tortillas. They always kept some of the corn seed for the next season's planting.

Later, when wheat flour was introduced to the Alabama-Coushattas, they began making fry bread—a mixture of flour, baking powder salt, and water. The mixture was flattened into five-inch disks and deep-fried until it is golden brown. The fry bread could be eaten plain, or with butter and jam. Today, some families prefer to put meat or weiners inside and cook the fry bread as the main course of their meal.

Fry bread can be eaten at the Inn of the Twelve Clans, a restaurant on the reservation. Visitors can also enjoy Indian tacos. These are made with fry bread and topped with a large helping of ground beef, cheese, lettuce, and tomatoes.

In the 1800s, the Alabama-Coushattas were known to have cattle, horses, and hogs. They also hunted for wild game in the Big Thicket, never going very far from their village. They hunted deer, turkey, and quail. Rivers and creeks in the Big Thicket provided fish, which was cooked over an open fire.

CLOTHING

Little is known about the kind of clothing worn by the Alabama-Coushattas before they came to Texas. We do know they fashioned their clothing from animal skins. The men wore garments that looked like long shirts, and the women had dresses similar to Roman togas. When the weather was cold, both men and women put their moccasins away and wore long, soft boots. By the time they settled along the Neches and Trinity rivers, they had adopted commercial cotton for most of their clothing.

Today the Alabama-Coushattas dress in the style of other Americans. The young people enjoy jeans, tee-shirts, and tennis shoes. They like bright colors and enjoy decorating plain clothing with ribbons and braids. The women wear skirts and blouses, dresses and slacks. The men wear clothing that is suitable for their jobs.

The traditional clothing of their ancestors is worn only during ceremonial dances and at Indian Pow Wows at the reservation and other parts of the country. The handmade outfits with their beautiful beading and interesting designs are very expensive.

SHELTER

The Alabama-Coushattas lived in houses made of logs. Tall pine trees growing in the Big Thicket were plentiful, and the Indians used them wisely. Trees were cut, and the logs shaped to build the cabins. The rectangular-shaped houses were then covered with thatch or bark.

Their first log houses had dirt floors. They did not have a fireplace so fires were built in the center of the home. There were two small vent holes in the roof so the smoke could escape, and fresh air could enter the cabins. Later the smoke hole was moved to the eaves of the house. This allowed the smoke to escape, but kept rain from drowning out their fires. By the time the Alabama-Coushattas were established in Texas they were building chimneys of clay and moss on one end of the cabin to replace the smoke holes.

The homes were grouped around a central house called the Council House, which was the meeting place for the tribe. All religious ceremonies and council meetings were held in the central house and still are today. No English is spoken during the council meetings, only the language of the Alabama-Coushattas.

The chief decided on the location of any house in

the tribe as well as the fields and orchards. He made sure family groups were kept near each other.

Family members and friends joined together to build the houses. While the men cut the trees, dried the logs, cut and split the shingles, mixed clay and moss for the chimneys, the women came to share the cooking. They made large pots of sofkey, beans, fry bread, and a mixture of corn and pork called pashofa.

Many modern frame houses and over one hundred brick homes have been built on the reservation, and more are being planned for the future.

WEAPONS AND TOOLS

The Alabama-Coushattas used the bow and arrow for hunting wild game in the Big Thicket. Arrowheads were made from flint or petrified wood. They were made in several sizes to fit different sized arrows.

Small game was hunted with a blow gun, which ranged in length from five to eight feet long. Long cane poles were sectioned and drilled to remove the inner joints. When iron rods were used, they were heated on the end and the joints burned out. The dart was made from cane slivers.

Long wooden poles with chipped flint or bone fastened to the end were used for digging in the crops. A stone axe was made by using large rocks for the cutting edge. Later, cultivators, hay rakes, and wheelbarrows were used on the reservation. Slingshots were also used when hunting small game such as rabbits, squirrels, and raccoons.

CUSTOMS AND RELIGION

Families of the Alabama-Coushattas formed clans. These clans came together in larger groups called phratries and moities. Members of the clans worked together and aided each other when necessary.

Each village had a leader, called the micco, who was chosen for his wisdom. He appointed a warrior chief who was in charge of any problems the clan might have with other Indian tribes or white settlers. The position of the micco was not handed down through the family, but was voted on by the clan.

The Alabama-Coushattas believed the creator was the master of life who breathed life into everything in the universe. They believed in good and evil spirits. Dances and ceremonies were very important to them, and the shaman was both a healer and a religious leader for the clans. Their main god was called Abba Mingo, the Great Chief of Earth and Sky.

In the early 1800s, the Alabama-Coushatta villages were centered around the meeting house, which was used as a council house and as a temple. One of their main ceremonies was held when the mulberry was ripe. The mulberries and other ripe fruits were placed in the open area and for several days thanks was offered to the spirits of the fruits and to their gods. Later the fruits were eaten by the people.

The first missionary movement among the Alabama-Coushattas was through the Presbyterian Church in 1881. When the missionaries arrived in the village, they found that only one man had a bible, which he could not read.

The missionaries were not allowed to live on the reservation. The Indians told them that General Sam Houston had been a wonderful friend to them and that he had advised them never to let a white man live on the reservation. No matter how much the missionaries pleaded, the Indians would not budge. So, the missionaries built a home outside the reservation and traveled many miles by horse and buggy to the reservation. However, the Indians were not interested in the new religion and preferred to continue their Fruit Festivals and other dances and ceremonies.

By the late 1800s, the missionary work was expanded, and as many as one hundred Alabama-Coushatta Indians attended the Presbyterian Church on the reservation.

Today, Alabama-Coushattas attend the Baptist, Presbyterian, and Assembly of God churches. They also continue to practice their traditional ceremonies, including the sacred pipe and eagle feather ceremonies. Visitors to the reservation can see the performance of such traditional dances as the Buffalo Dance, Victory Dance, and Dance of the Shawls. These dances are taught to children at a very early age so they can learn about their heritage and show pride in their traditions.

Marriage ceremonies among these Indians were quite simple. When a couple decided to marry, it had to be approved by the chief. The young man and the chief chose where the groom would build his house and cultivate corn and other crops. When the house was completed, the groom went to the home of the bride, took her hand and together they went to their new home. There was no ceremony, no dance or festival to celebrate the marriage of the two young people. However, records show that there were very few broken marriages among the Alabama-Coushattas.

CRAFTS

The Alabama-Coushattas have always been noted for their basket making. Longleaf pine needles are used to weave the baskets in a variety of shapes and sizes. The pine needles are best if they are gathered during wet weather when they are less brittle. If they are too dry, it becomes necessary for them to be dampened before work on the basket begins. The pine needles are made into coils which are wound into a basket shape. Then they are lashed together with raffia. The baskets are small because making them is very slow work.

Working fulltime, no more than three small baskets can be made in one day. Some of the baskets are made into birds and animals, and each has a perfectly fitted lid. Sometimes pinecone pieces are made into beads and woven into the basket.

Some baskets can be purchased at the gift shop, but many of them are used in the Alabama-Coushatta homes. They are used as decorative pieces in the home, as well as storage containers for dried foods. The baskets are also used to sift hand ground corn before it is cooked.

In earlier days baskets were made from split rivercane but few women know how to make these baskets today. The cane was more difficult to get than the pine needles. Then it had to be split very carefully and soaked for a long period of time before the weaving could begin. When finished, a rivercane basket was woven so tightly it could hold water.

Rugs, mats, and blankets were woven from Spanish moss. The moss was pulled from the large oak trees in the forest and dried until it turned black. A loom was made by hammering pegs into a board. Then the thick pieces of moss were twisted on the loom and made into coarse thread.

Pottery made by the Alabama-Coushattas was created of clay dug from the forest. When the clay was dry, it was ground between two stones until it changed into powder. When there were no lumps left in the clay, water was added. The clay was coiled to form bowls and pots, and then left in the sun to dry. Later they were placed in a burning pit to allow the "firing" to make them much stronger so they could be used for cooking.

Each piece was decorated by hand before it was "fired." Geometric lines and X's, or pictures of animals and birds were favorite designs. Bright colors and glazes were added to make the pottery last longer.

Beading was also popular among the Alabama-Coushattas. In the early days they traded skins and furs to the French for colorful beads. Beading today is done on a loom, sometimes directly on the leather and sometimes on other kinds of materials.

Jewelry is made from different kinds of seeds, including chinaberry and watermelon seeds. These seeds must be cleaned and boiled before they can be used. Sometimes they are dyed to add a variety of color. In the early days they boiled maple roots to make purple dye and walnuts to make a dark brown.

CHILDREN

The Alabama-Coushatta children were taught the ways of their people by their parents. There were no schools for them to attend, and because there was no written language it was not necessary for them to learn to read. Since the language was spoken and not written, it was necessary for boys and girls to develop good memories. By remembering family myths and stories, they continued the history of their people. Both boys and girls learned the myths and folk tales handed down by their ancestors. They practiced and performed the traditional dances of their people at an early age.

Boys learned to clear land and plant crops. They worked in the fields until the hunting season and then the work was left for the women and girls. Girls learned to weave baskets and prepare family meals.

Today, children living on the reservation attend public schools in nearby Woodville, Livingston, and Big Sandy. There is also a Head Start program on the reservation. Some students attend Haskell Indian Junior College in Kansas, as well as colleges and universities in New Mexico and Arizona. Those who choose to stay closer to home, usually attend Angelina Junior College in Lufkin, or Sam Houston State University in Huntsville.

112

CONCLUSION

Though the Alabama-Coushatta Indians still live on their reservation in southeast Texas, many of them attend school and work in nearby cities. The reservation is operated by the tribal council. Money received from oil production, government support, and tourism is used to maintain the reservation. It also helps pay for road and building repairs, and medical expenses for the people. No one owns their own land on the reservation, but it can be leased from the tribe. Each family is responsible for their own living expenses.

Until 1937, when they decided upon a written constitution, the chief had almost complete power of the tribe. Even after the constitution the tribe still had a chief and a second chief, but the power was given to the Tribal Council. The Tribal Council has seven members chosen by the people. It works with the Texas Commission for Indian Affairs and decides on any changes to be made for the tribe.

A tribal chief is elected for life. Fulton Battise became chief of the Alabama-Coushattas in a special ceremony on January 1, 1970. He served as their chief until his death in 1994. A new chief could not be elected until January 1, 1995.

Today the chief is mostly a ceremonial chief. His duties can be compared to those of a city mayor.

You must be born an Alabama-Coushatta Indian in order to belong to the tribe. If a marriage takes place with a member of another tribe, the other Indian must be adopted by the Alabama-Coushattas. They must show proof they are Indian, and then their name is placed on a ballot to be voted on during the next annual election. If there is a marriage with someone who is not an Indian, they may not live on the reservation. They remain a member of the tribe but have no voting rights.

Women of the tribe have as many rights as men

and are allowed to vote and own property. They may also serve on the Tribal Council. Carol Battise was the first woman to serve on the council.

The Alabama-Coushattas have been able to maintain their identity in the modern world. The native language of the Alabama and Coushattas is still spoken in their homes as well as during Tribal Council meetings. Over the years, with the two tribes working together, differences between the two languages is beginning to disappear.

The Tiguas

The Tigua (TEE gwah) Indians of El Paso are known as the oldest ethnic group in Texas.

Before Spanish explorers came to America, Tiwa-speaking Pueblo Indians lived along the Rio Grande Valley from northern Mexico to West Texas. When the Spanish came, they saw many adobe villages and called them pueblos.

The Spanish forced the Indians to be under the Catholic Church and made them build a mission at Isleta, New Mexico. The Spanish took the Indian's land and forced them to work in the mines. Soon the Indians rebelled and began attacking Spanish communities in New Mexico. Those Spaniards who were able to escape took 317 Tigua, (the Spanish spelling for Tiwa) Indians with them and fled down the Rio Grande. They stopped on the north side of the river and named their new home Ysleta del Sur, known as Isleta of the South. Today the land next to the church has been farmed since 1682. It is said to be the oldest cultivated land in Texas.

In 1871, when a law was passed to allow land to be sold to white settlers, the Tiguas lost most of their land. For several generations the Tiguas lived in poverty, and some feared their culture had disappeared.

In 1955, the city of El Paso annexed Ysleta, and the Tiguas had to pay taxes on their property. Since most

115

taxes amounted to $100 a year, and the average yearly income for a Tigua family was only $400, it was impossible for the taxes to be paid. With valuable legal aid and help from local officials, the Tiguas were finally recognized as a state and a national Native American Indian Tribe in 1968.

FOOD

The Tigua Indians farmed the land and raised corn, tomatoes, squash, beans, and other crops. They also had grapevines and orchards.

They hunted antelope, buffalo and deer, as well as small game such as rabbits and squirrels. Fishing along the Rio Grande supplemented their diets.

Bread was baked daily in a pueblo style "horno." A horno was a beehive-shaped outdoor oven heated with mesquite roots. A long, wooden paddle was used to bring the crusty loaves of Tigua Indian bread from the oven. The bread was brown and crunchy on the outside and soft and chewy on the inside. These large ovens are still being used on the reservation today, and when the oven doors are opened and the fresh smell of Indian bread fills the air, visitors make their way to the gift shop to purchase some of this delicious bread.

For four centuries or more red and green chili peppers have been used in Pueblo Indian cooking. The Spaniards brought them to New Mexico in the 1500s. The Tigua Indians began stringing dried peppers in their homes to be used for cooking. Vegetables from the garden were cooked with small amounts of chopped chili. A red chili paste was made by grinding dried chili pods on a metate with water and salt. This paste was spread on wild game for additional flavor.

Even today the Tiguas are very proud of their red chili, but nothing compares to their green chili, which is especially hot. Some have compared eating a bowl of green chili to chewing a bowl of fire.

Restaurants in the Tigua Indian Arts and Crafts Center offer a variety of Tex-Mex foods. These include chicken and beef fajitas, Indian burgers, tortilla soup, hot chili rellenos, and gorditas. Gorditas are made by stuffing ground beef, lettuce, tomatoes, and cheese into a cornmeal patty that has been deep-fried.

CLOTHING

When the Spanish explorers came in contact with the Tigua Indians, they found them wearing clothes made mainly from cotton. Some were trimmed with leather made from cowhide, and their coats were decorated with an assortment of turkey feathers.

Now, at the Tigua Indian Reservation you can see dancers in the traditional dress of their people. Young men wear brightly colored, cotton pullover shirts decorated with embroidery or beadwork. An embroidered belt, or cummerbund, is worn around the waist and hangs from the front to the knees. Knee-high moccasins are about two inches below their white kilt-like skirts. The moccasins have a row of silver bells sewn across the top. A matching headband is worn across the forehead.

The girls wear black dresses and shawls trimmed with embroidery, with an embroidered belt at the waist. They also wear moccasins that come to the knee.

SHELTER

When the Tigua Indians came to Texas, they built their villages along the Rio Grande. Their homes were called pueblos and were made of adobe bricks. These bricks were made from a mixture of clay, dried grasses, and ashes. When the mixture was thick enough, it was poured into a wooden frame and left in the sun to dry for several weeks. These adobe bricks made the walls very thick and kept the house cooler during the hottest time of the year. Today, workers sometimes add lime to the mixture to make the bricks more waterproof and durable.

In the early days rooms at ground level had no doors, and the family entered through an opening in the roof called a hatchway. This was done for protection since ladders could be taken up quickly in case of an attack. The roof was made by laying medium-size poles across the short side of the house. On top of this were smaller poles, split slabs, then brush, grass or leaves. The last layer was made of adobe. If more stories were added to the pueblo, the roof became the floor for the next level.

Firepits were built in the center of the room or against one wall and were used for cooking. There were no chimneys and the smoke escaped through the hatchway in the roof. Later, corner fireplaces with chimneys were introduced to the Tiguas.

In the 1540s they lived in four-story pueblos with ceremonial kivas. The kivas were used as a meeting place for the men and for various ceremonies. They were set apart from the main buildings and were entered through a roof hatchway and ladder.

Today, the Tigua Indians still live in their pueblo homes in the historic Mission district, about fifteen miles southwest of downtown El Paso. The main area covers 27.8 acres of land. Also on the reservation is a 113 unit housing community.

WEAPONS AND TOOLS

The Tiguas believed their hunting grounds were given to them by the gods. When they went hunting, it was not just to get meat for the tribe, but to honor the memory of their ancestors.

When they hunted for jackrabbits, they used long wooden sticks with sharp points. This weapon was like the ancient spears hunters used before they knew how to make spearheads of stone or flint. Even now the Tiguas do not use guns for hunting rabbits, and they still use the long, wooden sticks.

In earlier days the war captain was in charge of all the hunting for the tribe. He still is today. However, modern weapons are now used. The hunters have rifles, buckshot guns, and modern army surplus guns. When the war captain gives the command, the men and boys go into the desert to hunt. They go in cars, trucks, and the tribal station wagon. Every hunter has his own gun. The war captain is sure the prayers have been said and that the hunt has been properly blessed before leaving the reservation. The hunting done today is a method of recreation rather than a means of survival.

CUSTOMS AND RELIGION

When the Tiguas were driven from New Mexico, they brought with them to Texas their canes of authority. These were metal-topped canes that had been presented to the Tigua leaders by the Spanish government.

When the Tiguas were separated from their relatives in the north, the missionaries forced them to build the Ysleta Mission near El Paso. The mission still stands today. The foundation and a large part of the adobe walls in the mission today were built by the Tiguas two hundred years ago. Even though the church was heavily damaged by fire and other disasters through the years, it has been in constant use since 1682.

The mission was dedicated to Saint Anthony, and the Tiguas had brought with them a statue of Saint Anthony. When the church was completed, the statue was placed in the church and remains as the patron saint of the Tigua Indians. Each year on June 13, they celebrate Saint Anthony's Day as their main religious holiday. On this day the saint's statue is carried through the streets to the church. For this one occasion, the chief of the Tiguas serves as their priest. As a symbol he lashes the people with willow switches for their sins.

In ancient times they believed the sun was the father of life on earth, because nothing could grow without the sun. So, the Tiguas prayed to the Father Sun who sent his warmth to nourish Mother Earth.

Present-day Tiguas have been able to blend Roman Catholicism with their own traditional religion. Celebrations and dances are held throughout the year as they combine their feast days with those celebrations of the Catholic church. In this way they are able to work well with the Spanish and Mexican clergy, without giving up the chants, ceremonies, and drums that are so much a part of their culture. The Tiguas, like many other Texas tribes, also believe in the shaman.

On New Year's Eve the people elect their governor, lieutenant governor, and bailiff. They also elect four captains to act as assistants to the war captain during ceremonial dances. Three people are then elected to be in charge of the fiesta of Saint Anthony.

Tiwa, the native language of the Tiguas is no longer in common use. However, the tribal elders still speak the language and are making an attempt to pass it down to the younger generation so it will not be lost forever.

In the desert area there are many hidden valleys and deep caves. One such hidden valley contains secret waterholes and ancient cave writings. The Tiguas believe it is a sacred place, and they have named it "Hueco." The shallow caves and overhangs in the rocks are covered with pictographs. One shows dancing figures carrying musical instruments. Another rock overhang was a favorite Tigua camping spot in 1894, and some Tigua Indians have written their names there.

Even today the Tiguas believe in living as one large family. Within the tribe, when a man has good fortune he is expected to share with those who are less fortunate or he is considered to be selfish.

They also share their way of life and their beliefs, their joys and their pains. If someone in the tribe is sick, everyone is expected to help. They bring food, and they pray. If someone in the tribe has good fortune and is happy, everyone comes to share that happiness.

CRAFTS

Tigua pottery was made in the ancient Pueblo way. This was done by rolling coils or "snakes" of clay. A flat piece of clay, like a pancake, was used for the bottom of the pot. Then the rolled "snakes" were layered around the edge of the bottom. They built up the sides of the pot by coiling the "snakes" around until the pot was the height they desired. The sides were smoothed and the pot left to dry in the sun for several days. Then a coating of colored clay and water was painted over the pot. When this dried, it was polished by rubbing the pot with a smooth stone. Designs painted on the pottery pieces were like those found in ancient pictographs on the cave walls in the Hueco Tanks east of El Paso. When the pottery was completed, it was fired to make it more durable. This was done by cooking it under a pile of slowly burning, dried manure.

The Tiguas still make pottery on the reservation today and some red clay from the Hueco Mountains is still used. Visitors can watch demonstrations of painting techniques. Pottery can be purchased at the gift shop as a reminder of this Tigua craft.

At the Living Arts Pueblo, which is a replica of a Pueblo community, you can see artists weaving blankets, belts, and many other items. Other artifacts, such as pipes and axes, are also made there.

CHILDREN

Tigua children learned at an early age how to do their part in the family life.

When a Tigua boy lost a tooth, he would throw it high in the sky, toward the sun. He believed the sun made things grow. Therefore, the sun would grow him a new tooth. He threw the tooth back-handed because he did not want the tooth to be disrespectful and hit the sun.

Young boys were also taught to play the tribal drum. The drumbeats had to be practiced and learned by heart, since there was no written music. The fathers taught their sons, and when the time came the sons would teach their sons.

Today, some Tigua boys practice by playing on an empty gas tank of a junked car, which they beat with their fists. Pebbles are placed in empty cans to be used as rattles.

Now Tigua children dress in the same kinds of clothing worn by children from other parts of Texas. However, they dress in the traditional costume of their tribe to perform dances for visitors several times a day during the summer. Tigua children are taught the dances and rituals of the tribe so their heritage will not be lost.

They attend school and speak English, but they practice the language of their people at home.

CONCLUSION

After escaping to Texas during the Pueblo Revolt in 1680, the Tigua Indians have lived quietly and peaceably in Texas for the past three centuries. They served as scouts for the United States Calvary and the Texas Rangers during Indian Wars and did so until the last fight with the Apaches took place in 1881.

In 1955, life for the Tiguas became much more difficult. Ysleta was made a part of El Paso, and taxes on their homes were raised so high they could not pay them.

When the people in El Paso and other parts of Texas learned about the problems of the Tiguas, they offered their help. Finally, on April 12, 1968, the federal government recognized the Tiguas as an official Indian tribe. They were the last tribe to receive official recognition by the United States.

No matter how hard things were for the Tiguas, they never gave up their spirit as a people, and they clung to their heritage. Today the Tiguas are no longer a forgotten people, and they continue to make progress each year.

The Kickapoos

Present-day Kickapoo (Kik a POO) Indians live in their summer homes along the Rio Grande near Eagle Pass. They spend their winters in El Nacimiento, Mexico, near the headwaters of the Rio Sabinas. This is about eight miles southwest of Eagle Pass.

The Kickapoos were first noticed by explorers near the Great Lakes region in 1640. Gradually they were pushed farther west then south. One group moved to the Sabine River in Texas, where they became friends with the Cherokee Chief Bowles.

When Texas gained its independence from Mexico, the Kickapoo tribes divided once more. One band went to Indian Territory, in present-day Oklahoma, and the other band went to Mexico.

For many years the Kickapoos guarded the Mexican border against Comanches and Apaches. The Mexicans were so thankful for their help at the border, they gave the Kickapoos 17,000 acres of land.

The Kickapoos began to raid white settlers in Texas. The raids continued, and the Texas government was determined to send the Kickapoos to Indian Territory with other members of their tribe. In 1873, while Kickapoo warriors were away from their families, a United States military patrol kidnapped all the women, children, and elderly men they could find and took them to Indian Territory. Within the next five years over six hundred Kickapoos had moved northward to Oklahoma.

They were not happy with reservation life, and they resisted giving up their traditional way of life. By the late 1800s about two-thirds of the Kickapoos had left Oklahoma and returned to the Rio Grande. They moved freely across the Mexican and United States border.

During the 1940s there was a drought in Mexico, which created problems for the Kickapoos. In order to survive they became migrant workers, following the harvests as far as the Dakotas. They lived on a campground on the north bank of the Rio Grande at Eagle Pass, which was underneath the International Bridge.

The United States government wanted them to return to their relatives in Oklahoma. The Mexican government urged them to live on the lands they had given them, but the Kickapoos refused to leave. Therefore, the Kickapoos were not citizens of either country. This meant they had no education, health, or job-training programs that were being provided for recognized Indian tribes.

By 1978, the Texas legislature finally recognized the Kickapoo Indians as an Indian nation, and they became known as the Kickapoo Traditional Tribe of Texas.

Today the Kickapoo Indians have two settlements. They have 125 acres of land near Eagle Pass and another settlement in Coahuila, Mexico. This gives them joint citizenship with the United States and Mexico.

FOOD

The Kickapoos were primarily farmers. When there was enough rain for crops they planted corn, squash, beans, and melons. They also gathered roots and berries to supplement their diet.

Corn was crushed with a wooden mortar and pestle

and then boiled. Fry bread, which was made with wheat flour, salt, and baking soda, was fried in deep fat.

They hunted for deer, rabbits, squirrels, and other small animals for their meat supply. In earlier times they also hunted buffalo. For the buffalo hunts they used the "surround" method. Sometimes they would set fires to frighten the buffalo, causing them to stampede.

CLOTHING

The traditional clothing for the Kickapoo was made of cotton. The men wore long, full-sleeved shirts and cotton pants. They sometimes wore silver bracelets on the outside of their shirts just above the elbows. Vests were very popular with the Kickapoo, and they were decorated with beads, shells, and seeds.

A variety of headpieces were worn, including fur hats with feathers attached to the back. They wore all kinds of feathers on their head, from one single feather, to a headdress with feathers sticking straight up around the head. Wide-brimmed cloth hats were also a favorite of the tribe.

Moccasins were worn by all tribe members. Some were made from plain buckskin, and others were decorated with brightly-colored beads.

SHELTER

The Kickapoo Indians traditionally lived in villages. They had a summer home and a winter home. These homes were oval-shaped wigwams.

The framework of both homes was made from long, slender poles. The summer home was covered with bark from an elm or birch tree. The floor was sometimes covered with reed mats, but many times it was left bare. A platform along the inside wall of the home was used for a place to sit or sleep. To add more warmth to the winter home the floors were covered with mats made of grass and reeds.

126

When it came time to build a wigwam, a rectangular floor area was marked off first. Then several holes were dug along the outline that had been marked. When the holes were deep enough, the bottom of a springy pole was placed in each of the holes. Then one man reached up and pulled one of the poles downward and inward while another man pulled down the top of the pole opposite it. As one held the poles in place, the other lashed the tops of the poles together with strips of roots or fibers. This continued until all the poles were lashed, and the large, oval-shaped frame was completed. Then more saplings were lashed to the framework, some going over the roof and others around the sides.

The door always faced east and was covered with animal skins. In the middle of the floor a shallow pit was dug for the fire. The pit was surrounded by flat rocks. A smoke hole in the top of the wigwam allowed the smoke to escape. In order to keep the fire going day and night many Kickapoos used the "star fire" method. A small fire was built in the center of the pit. When the fire began to blaze, five long logs were placed around the fire. They were arranged like a five-pointed star, with one end of each log in the fire. As the logs burned down, they were pushed into the fire. On very cold or stormy nights the grandmother or grandfather stayed up to tend the fire.

When the Kickapoos first came to Texas, they lived in modernized wigwams under the International Bridge at Eagle Pass. They built their wigwams out of wood and cardboard, using rush mats to cover them.

WEAPONS AND TOOLS

A stone-headed club and sharp stick were used by the Kickapoos. With these tools they dug holes for poles that would make the framework for their homes.

In earlier times they used the bow and arrow for

hunting small game. They also used traps for small animals. A "deer call" was made by carving a small oval piece of wood which they attached to a piece of rawhide. When they blew into the deer call, it made a sound similar to that of a deer. The deer followed the call into the open area and became an easy target for the hunters.

Later, animal skins were traded to the white man for hatchets, knives, guns, and gun powder.

CUSTOMS AND RELIGION

A Kickapoo family always included the grandparents. The grandfather told stories of Indian life, tales of bravery by members of the tribe, and the importance of good deeds. He wanted to keep the traditions of the tribe alive for the younger members of the tribe.

The Kickapoos resisted foreign cultures. They shunned the religious beliefs of other people and refused to go to the missions. Clinging to their own religious ceremonies and customs they tried to avoid all other religions.

Festivals began early in the year when the first thunder was heard. This was usually sometime in February. With the coming of spring, the Kickapoos prepared their summer home and opened the sacred medicine bundles. A month or more of celebrations followed, which included personal and family feasts, naming the new babies, or remembering the death of someone in the family. The Corn Dance was celebrated in late July or August. Dancers for the celebration wore ceremonial clothes, and each carried an object which they waved to the rhythm of the drums. The winter homes were prepared during the fall of the year. During this celebration the bundles were tied up, and activities were centered around the family. The winters were spent hunting and telling myths and stories about the tribe.

There were four sacred bundle societies of the

Kickapoo Indians. Their main ceremonies took place in February. During this time the bundles of deerskin holding pipes, beads, and flutes were opened.

Today the people wear their traditional costumes during the ceremonies. These costumes include a breechcloth, moccasins, leggings, and long-sleeved white shirts.

The present-day religious beliefs of the Kickapoos are changing. About one-third of the tribe belong to a Protestant Church. Another one-third belong to both Protestant and tribal faiths. The rest of the tribe either belong to a Native American Church or continue to practice only the tribal faith. Most of those who follow the tribal faith are the older members of the tribe.

For many years no one married outside the tribe. Today, more and more are marrying other Native Americans from surrounding areas. Therefore, as the years go by, there will be fewer and fewer full-blooded Kickapoo Indians.

CRAFTS

Most crafts done by the Kickapoos were made of wood and were useful to the tribe. They made cradleboards, bowls, and deer calls. They carved ladles to be used for dipping into the large pots of stew. Many of these were decorated with carvings and porcupine quills. The Kickapoos also weaved baskets of all sizes.

CHILDREN

The children were taught the traditions and stories of the tribe by their grandfather. They learned the skills of everyday life from their parents.

For many years the children were denied an education because the Kickapoos resisted educating their children with the white man. They did not want them to lose their identity or give up their traditions and cus-

toms. However, by the 1970s most of the children were attending local schools.

Now, financial aid is being given to those who choose to attend college or seek a trade. Many of the children are bilingual, speaking both Spanish and the Algonquian language of their people. Most of them also speak English.

CONCLUSION

The Kickapoos are considered one of the most traditional Indian tribes in the United States. They refuse to give up their customs and religion, and they continue to practice ceremonies and rituals from the past.

The population of the Kickapoos in Texas varies from season to season as they move back and forth across the border.

They are working hard to improve their way of life by including health-care services, better roads, and an adequate water system. They are now building homes on their land and educating their children.

Other Texas Tribes

Some Indian tribes lived in Texas for a short period of time. These included the Delaware, Cherokee, Seminole, and Shawnee.

THE DELAWARES

The Delaware Indians crossed the Red River into Texas between 1815 and 1820. Most of them settled near the Caddo Indians because they felt a real kinship with this tribe. They soon began wearing clothing like the white man, believing this was a better way of getting along with the settlers.

The Delawares wanted more than just to survive. They wanted schools and teachers for their children. They wanted a place for sharing goods and buying products. By 1828, the Delawares had made Nacogdoches their trading center.

They knew it was important to have title to their land. However, after Texas won its independence from Mexico, more and more settlers came to Texas and took the Indian's land.

In 1839, their friends, the Cherokees, were charged with helping the Mexicans during the Texas Revolution. For two days a battle between the Cherokees and Delawares on one side, and the Texas Army on the other was fought. The army drove the Indians back across the

Red River to Oklahoma, and their lands were sold to white settlers.

Many Delawares refused to return to Oklahoma and joined other Indians at the headwaters of the Pedernales River. No matter how hard they tried, they found it difficult to raise crops and survive in the Hill Country.

When the Brazos Reserve was established for the Indians, many Delawares became a part of that reservation. In spite of their efforts to make life on the reservation work, pressure from white settlers caused the Delaware to move, and once more the Delawares crossed the Red River into Oklahoma.

THE CHEROKEES

The Cherokee Indians came to Texas in the 1820s after being forced out of Georgia. They built their homes north of Nacogdoches.

Sam Houston had lived with the Cherokee Indians in Tennessee for three years and knew their language, customs, and way of life. He also lived among the Cherokees in Arkansas, and later he married an Indian girl named Tiana Rogers.

Because he knew and understood the Cherokees, Sam Houston was constantly trying to make relations between the Cherokees and the settlers more peaceful. During the Texas Revolution, Houston was sent to make a treaty with the tribe, stating that the Cherokees would remain peaceful throughout the Revolution. Texas promised the Cherokees they would have title to their land if this treaty was honored. After the Battle of San Jacinto, the newly formed Republic of Texas failed to honor the agreement they had made with the Cherokees, and more and more settlers took over their land.

When Mirabeau Lamar became president of the Republic of Texas, his feelings toward the Cherokees and other Indian tribes was the opposite of Sam

Houston's. In a speech to Congress in 1839, Lamar stated:

> The white man and the red man cannot dwell in harmony together. Nature forbids it . . . if peace can be obtained only by the sword, let the sword do its work.

Lamar believed the Cherokees had no claim to their land, and in the summer of 1839, he ordered them out of Texas. Chief Bowles, leader of the Cherokees, asked for time to gather their crops and try to find peaceful solutions to their problems. Lamar would not listen.

On July 16, General Kelsey Douglass led the Texas Rangers in an attack on the Cherokees. The attack took place on the Neches River near present-day Tyler. A few Texans, and about one hundred Cherokees were killed in the battle. One of the first to be killed was Chief Bowles, who died proudly wearing the sash and sword given him by his friend, Sam Houston.

Those Cherokees who survived the battle were driven off their land. Most of them moved across the Red River to Indian Territory, which later became the state of Okahoma.

One of the most important achievements of the Cherokee Indians was the invention of the Cherokee alphabet. In the early 1900s, a man named Sequoyah dreamed of having a "talking leaf" like the white man. After twelve years of persistence and hard work, he had constructed a syllabic alphabet that could be learned in two or three days. There were eighty-five symbols in this alphabet and each symbol represented a sound in the Cherokee spoken language. Sequoyah presented it to the tribal chiefs and won their approval.

With this alphabet the Cherokees had the ability to communicate, which helped them to became a more literate people. In 1827, type was made for each letter and the first Indian press was established in America. A year later printing was done in English and in Cherokee.

Today most of the Cherokees speak and write English. However, some of the older generation prefer to speak their native language. Efforts are being made to keep the language alive by teaching it through special classes.

THE SHAWNEES

The Shawnee Indians entered the United States from lands north of the Great Lakes region. They settled in Pennsylvania, Illinois, Virginia, Maryland, and some as far south as Alabama. During the French and Indian Wars, some of the Shawnees moved to Indiana and Missouri.

Early in the nineteenth century Tecumseh's brother, Tenskwatawa, led the Shawnee to the mouth of Tippecanoe River, Indiana. General Harrison led a battle against the Shawnees, and in 1811 defeated them in the famous Battle of Tippecanoe. The following year the tribe's recognized leader, Tecumseh, died.

In 1825, the Shawnees in Missouri sold their land to the government and were assigned to a reservation in Kansas. However, many of them left for Texas and settled on the headwaters of the Sabine River.

The Shawnee Indians were considered to be an active, cheerful, creative, and courageous tribe. Because they had lived in so many places, the Shawnees could speak several different languages.

By 1839, the Shawnee Indians had left Texas and moved to Indian Territory in present-day Oklahoma.

THE SEMINOLES

The word Seminole means "one who leaves his tribe." The name was first given to the Creek Indians who left their homes in Georgia and moved further south to Florida. Later, Negro slaves who had run away from the plantation owners came to Florida, too. These Indians and Negroes lived together, worked together, and married each other. This combination of Creek Indians, Negro Slaves, and the Florida Indians became known as the Seminole Indians.

The Seminoles are best remembered for their two wars with the United States. The first was a short conflict from 1817–1818. The second, known as the Seminole War lasted seven years, beginning in 1835 and ending in 1842. It was considered to be the worst war ever waged against the Indians by the United States.

The Seminoles were fighting to keep their land and refused to be sent to Indian Territory in Oklahoma. The United States commissioners called the Indian chiefs together in May, 1835. When they presented them with a treaty that would force the Seminoles to leave Florida, the chiefs remained silent. Suddenly, a chief named Oscelo stepped forward, plunging his long knife into the treaty and stating, "This is our answer." Oscelo, the youngest of the group, had spoken for all the chiefs, and he became the new war leader.

Despite years of determination, fighting, and destruction the Seminoles were defeated by the United States. Some Seminoles escaped to the swamps, but most of them were sent to Indian Territory and placed on reservations. They became one of the Five Civilized Tribes of Oklahoma.

Most of the Seminoles who came to Texas associated themselves with the Cherokees in East Texas. At least one group is known to have gone into West Texas on hunting and trading expeditions.

Almost all the Seminoles who once lived in Texas moved further south into Mexico until the 1870s. Then, about five hundred of mixed Indian and Negro people came back into Texas and settled near Eagle Pass. A company of mounted scouts, stationed at Fort Clark, was organized from this group of Indians. They worked with the federal troops during 1874-1875 to remove the Plains Indians from West Texas.

A few of the original Seminole-Negro group still live in the vicinity of Bracketville, Texas. An Indian scout burial ground located in Bracketville has become a tourist attraction. Also, the town of Seminole, Texas, got its name from the nearby watering places of the Seminole Indians.

Glossary

ADOBE BRICKS — A mixture of earth, ashes, dried grasses, and water, used to make pueblos.

AGGRESSORS — Those who begin a fight.

ALABAMA-COUSHATTA — A tribe of Indians who now live on a reservation near Livingston.

ALLIGATOR GREASE — Used by the Indians to keep the mosquitoes away.

ANCESTOR — One from whom an individual is descended. A family member who lived long ago.

APACHE — A nomadic tribe of Indians in Texas.

ARBOR — A shelter formed of or covered with vines or branches. The Indians built them beside their homes.

ARCHAEOLOGICAL — The study of past human life as revealed by artifacts left behind.

ARCHAEOLOGIST — A scientist who studies artifacts left by the early people.

ARTIFACTS — Objects made and used by people of the past.

ATAKAPAN — A tribe of Indians in Texas who lived along the northern part of the Gulf Coast.

BAND — A group of Indians who lived together.

BEEHIVES — The Caddo Indians' homes, named for their shape.

BIG THICKET — The forest of East Texas and home of the Alabama-Coushatta Indians.

BILINGUAL — Knowing or using two languages.

BOBSEY — Cornmeal mush eaten by the Alabama-Coushatta Indians.

BOW AND ARROW — One of the main weapons used by the Indians.

BREECHCLOTH — A piece of material, similar to an apron, worn by Indian men. It is worn slightly longer in back than in front.

BUFFALO – A large, shaggy-maned North American animal that was very important to the Indians, providing their meat, clothing and shelter.

BUFFALO DOCTORS – A society in the Kiowa Indian tribe that treated diseases.

CABEZA DE VACA – A Spanish explorer. The first European to explore the interior of Texas.

CADDI – A Caddo Indian chief.

CADDO – A tribe of Indians that were located in the Piney Woods of East Texas. Texas got its name from the Caddo Indians.

CANES OF AUTHORITY – Canes given to the leaders of the Tigua Indians.

CHANT – To utter or repeat something over and over.

COAHUILTECAN – A tribe of Indians who lived inland from Galveston Bay to the Rio Grande. They are now extinct.

COMANCHE – A tribe of Indians who lived in the northern and western parts of Texas.

CORN DANCE – A celebration of the Indians.

COUNCIL HOUSE – A meeting place for the Indian tribe.

CRADLEBOARD – A thin board the Indians used for carrying their babies.

CULTURE – A particular stage or form of civilization. Culture includes a group of people's tools, clothing, music, art, religion, and other things.

CUSTOMS – A way of doing things that is shared by a group of people.

DEER CALL – A carved piece of wood attached to a piece of rawhide. The Indians used it when they were hunting for deer.

DESCENDANT – One descending from another. Coming from an ancestor.

DROUGHT – A long period of time without water rain.

EAGLE PASS – The summer home of the Kickapoo Indians, located along the Rio Grande.

EDWARDS PLATEAU – Large piece of high, flat land near Austin, Texas.

ETHNIC GROUP – A particular group of people who share the same customs and traits.

EXTINCT – Something that is no longer in existence.

FLACCO – A leader of the Apache Indians who was also a friend to the white man.

GERONIMO – A Chiricahua Apache chief.

GETTING READY TIME – When the Kiowa Indians built their ceremonial lodge.

GODDESS OF WATER – A goddess of the Wichita Indians. She provided the healing power of water for the people and for crops.

GORDITAS – Stuffed cornmeal patties made by the Tigua Indians.

HASINAI – The largest Caddo Confederacy. It is from this group that Texas got its name.

HERNANDO DE SOTO – The first Spanish explorer to meet the Alabama-Coushatta Indians.

HONEY EATERS – The largest Comanche band of Indians.

HORNO – An outdoor oven used by the Indians for baking bread.

HOUSTON, SAM – A friend to the Indians of Texas who served as governor for a time.

HUT – A small and sometimes temporary dwelling for the Indians.

INDIAN TERRITORY – An area where Indians were sent by the United States government. What is now the state of Oklahoma.

INTERNATIONAL BRIDGE – A bridge that separates two countries.

IRON SHIRT – A chief of the Comanche Indians. He was believed to have supernatural powers.

JERKY – Meat that is cured and dried in the sun. The Indians used buffalo meat for jerky.

JUMANO – An extinct tribe of Indians who lived along the Rio Grande near El Paso.

KARANKAWA – A tribe of Indians who lived from Galveston Bay southward along the coast to about Corpus Christi Bay. They are now extinct.

KICKAPOO – A tribe of Indians who lived part of the year along the Rio Grande near Eagle Pass, and the rest of the year in Mexico.

KINNIKASUS – The most important spirit of the Wichita Indians.

KIOWA – A tribe of Indians who settled in the Panhandle of Texas.

KIVA – A meeting place for men of the Tigua Indian tribe.

KWAHADIS – The most hostile band of Comanche Indians.

LADLE – A deep-bowled spoon with a long handle used for taking up and conveying liquids.

LANCE – A sharp-pointed weapon with long shafts.

LA SALLE – A French explorer who came in contact with the Caddo Indians.

LEGGINGS – A covering for the legs.

LITTLE CORN – The first corn that was planted each season.

LONE WOLF – An important chief of the Kiowa Indians.

LOOM – A frame used for weaving threads into cloth.

MAIZE – Corn grown by the Indians.

MAMAN-TI – A Kiowa chief who was known as the Owl Prophet.

MESCAL – A drink made from agave leaves.

MESQUITE BEAN – A thorny shrub with pods used as food for the Jumano Indians.

MICCO – Leader of an Alabama-Coushatta village.

MIDDENS – Old shell heaps.

MIGRANT WORKERS – People who move in order to find work. They follow the harvest and crops.

MITOTE – A religious ceremony practiced by the Coahuiltecan Indians.

MISSIONS – Settlements consisting of a church and other buildings, with the purpose of teaching the Indians about God.

MORTAR – A strong bowl in which substances are pounded or crushed with a pestle.

NOMADS – People who move from place to place.

PANHANDLE – A narrow projection of land at the top of Texas. The southeastern part of the Panhandle is about 900 meters (3,000 feet) high. By the time you get to the northwestern part of the Panhandle, some of the land is 1,380 meters (4,600 feet) high.

PARFLECHE – A rectangular-shaped box used by the Comanche Indians.

PARKER, CYNTHIA ANN – A nine-year-old Anglo girl captured by the Comanche Indians. She later married a Comanche chief, and her son became a chief.

PARKER, QUANAH – Son of Cynthia Ann Parker. The last chief of the Comanche Indians.

PEMMICAN – Food of the Plains Indians, consisting of dried buffalo meat, fat and juices, combined with berries, nuts, fruits or roots.

PETA NACONA – Chief of the Comanche Indians. He was the husband of Cynthia Ann Parker.

PICTOGRAPH — Picture writing done by the Indians to tell a story.

PINEY WOODS — The northeastern part of Texas. The home of the Caddo Indians.

PIROGUE — A dugout canoe.

PRAIRIE — A broad tract of flat or rolling grassland.

PRICKLY PEAR — A cactus plant that produces a pulpy pear-shaped, edible fruit.

PROPHET — A man of God who utters divinely inspired revelations.

PROTESTANT — A member of a Christian church.

PUEBLO — An Indian home made from adobe bricks.

QUIVER — A case for carrying arrows.

RABBIT SOCIETY — A society for Kiowa boys.

RABBIT STICK — A curved wooden stick used for hunting rabbits.

RAID — A sudden attack.

RACCOON-EYED PEOPLE — A name given to the Wichita Indians.

RESERVATIONS — Land that has been set aside for the Indians.

RITUALS — Certain acts undertaken in a religious ceremony.

RIVER PEOPLE — A name given to the Atakapan Indians.

SAINT ANTHONY'S DAY — The main religious holiday for the Tigua Indians.

SAPLINGS — Young trees.

SATANTA — A chief of the Kiowa Indians who brought fear to the white settlers. He was known as White Bear.

SCAFFOLD — A raised platform used for the Comanche dead.

SEINES — Large fishing nets.

SHAMAN — An Indian religious leader who is thought to use magic to cure the sick, and is able to reveal and control hidden events.

SHIELD — A thick piece of rawhide the Indians used for protection.

SINEW — The tendon of an animal.

SKIRMISH — A minor dispute. A small battle.

SOTOL — A wild plant eaten by the Apache Indians.

SOUTH STAR (— The guardian of the Wichita warriors.

STORYTELLER — A teller of stories. The storyteller taught the Wichita children about the gods.

STONE BOILING — A method of preparing food. The Jumanos heated stones, then picked them up with tongs made of sticks, and dropped them into a container partly filled with water. When the water started to boil, the food to be cooked was added.

SUN DANCE — A ceremonial dance that lasted twelve days.

SUCCOTASH — Beans, kernels of sweet corn, and other vegetables cooked together.

SUPERNATURAL — Of or pertaining to phenomena beyond or outside of what we consider to be natural.

TATTOOING — Piercing of the skin with pointed objects to make pictures on the skin.

TAYSHAS — A greeting from the Caddo Indians that meant "friendship."

TEEPEE — An Indian conical-shaped tent made of skins.

TEKNONYMY — The practice of naming the father after the child. It was used by the Atakapans.

TEXAS RANGERS — A group that enforced the law in early Texas, and continues to do so today.

THE TEN GRANDMOTHERS — Name given to the medicine bundles of the Kiowa Indians.

TIGUA — A tribe of Indians living in El Paso. They are known as the oldest ethnic group in Texas.

TINDE — The small family groups of the Apache Indians.

TIWA — The native language of the Tigua Indians.

TONKAWA — Indians who lived on the Edwards Plateau near present-day Austin. The name meant "they all stay together."

TORTILLAS — A round, thin cake of unleavened cornmeal bread.

TOTEMIC CLAN — A group composed of relatives.

TREATY — A written agreement.

TRIBE — A group of related people who have their own customs, traditions and way of life.

TRAVOIS — An A-shaped wooden frame pulled by dogs or horses and used to carry equipment and animal skins.

TRINKETS — Small ornaments, such as jewels or rings.

TROTLINE — A method of catching fish.

VANISH — To pass from sight or existence. To disappear.

VICTORIA — Chief of the Chiricahua Apache Indians.

VISION — Unusual wisdom in foreseeing what is going to happen in the future.

WAIL — To make a mournful cry.

WANDERERS — The most nomadic tribe of the Comanche Indians.

144

WAR CAPTAINS — Men in charge of all the hunting for the Tigua Indians.

WARRIOR SOCIETY — A type of police group for the Kiowa Indians.

WICHITA — A tribe of Indians who lived along the Red River. They settled near present-day Dallas and Fort Worth, and later in the vicinity of Waco.

WICKIUP — A hut used by nomadic Indians with an oval base and a rough frame covered with reedmats, grass, or brushwood.

WIGWAM — A hut used by the Kickapoo Indians. It was made with an arched framework of poles overlaid with bark, rush mats, or hides.

YAUPON — A plant used for making tea.

YSUN — The Apache god.

Bibliography

Adams, Carolyn. *Stars Over Texas,* Austin, TX: Eakin Press, 1983.

Anderson, Adrian, David G. Armstrong, Jeanie R. Stanley, Ralph A. Wooster. *Texas and Texans.* Lake Forest, IL: Macmillan/McGraw Hill, 1993.

Andrews, Elaine. *Indians of the Plains.* New York, NY: Facts on File, 1992.

Bleeker, Sonia. *The Seminole Indians.* New York, NY: William Morrow & Company, 1954.

Brandon, William. (Adapted for young readers by Anne Terry White). *The American Indian.* New York, NY: Random House, 1963.

Doherty, Craig. *The Apaches and Navajos.* New York, NY: Franklin Watts, 1989.

Doman, Wilson E. "Man in the Lower Pecos." *Texas Parks and Wildlife,* May 1981, Vol. 39, 2-5.

Eisen, Jonathan, and Harold Straugh. *Unknown Texans.* New York, NY: Macmillan Publishing Company, 1988.

Elbow, Gary S., Archie P. McDonald, Mary Garcia Metzer, and Rodolfo Rocha. *Texas Yesterday and Today.* Silver Burdett & Ginn, Inc., 1988.

Estep, Irene. *Seminoles.* Chicago: Melmont Publishers, Inc., 1963.

Fox, Vivian. *The Winding Trail.* Austin, TX: Eakin Press, 1983.

Frantz, Joe B., and James B. Kracht. *Texas The Study of Our State,* Scott Foresman and Company, Glenview, IL, 1988.

Freedman, Russell. *Buffalo Hunt.* New York, NY: Scholastic Publications, Inc., 1988.

———. *Indian Chiefs.* New York, NY: Scholastic Publications, Inc., 1987.

Haley, James L. *Apaches, A History and Culture Portrait.* Garden City, NY: Doubleday & Company, Inc., 1981.

Harston, J. Emmor. *Comanche Land.* San Antonio, TX: The Naylor Company, 1963.

Holt, Roy D. *Heap Many Texas Chiefs.* San Antonio, TX: The Naylor Company, 1966.

Hunt, W. Ben. *Indian Crafts and Lore.* New York: Golden Press, Western Publishing Inc., 1954.

Israel, Marion. *Apaches.* Chicago: Melmont Publishers, Inc., 1959.

———. *Cherokees.* Chicago: Melmont Publishers, Inc., 1961.

Jacobson, Daniel. *Great Indian Tribes.* Maplewood, NJ: Hammond, Inc., 1970.

Kownslar, Allan O. *The Texans Their Land and History.* New York: McGraw-Hill, 1978.

Leavitt, Dr. Jerome. *America and its Indians.* Chicago: Children's Press, 1962.

Lowry, Jack. "A Celebration of Cultures." *Texas Highways,* November 1991, pp. 42–49.

———. "The People." *Texas Highways,* July 1991, 47–52.

MacFarland, Allan A. *Book of American Indian Games.* New York: Association Press, 1958.

Malone, P. V. *Sam Houston's Indians: The Alabama-Coushatti.* San Antonio, TX: The Naylor Company, 1960.

Martin, Howard N. *Myths & Folktales of the Alabama-Coushatta Indians of Texas.* Austin, TX: The Encino Press, 1977.

McKissack, Patricia. *The Apache.* Chicago: Childrens Press, 1984.

Melody, Michael E. *The Apaches.* New York: Chelsea House Publishers, 1989.

Newcomb, W. W., Jr. *The Indians of Texas.* Austin, TX: University of Texas Press, 1961.

The New Book of Knowledge. New York: Grolier Inc., 1973.

Ney, Marian Wallace. *Indian Americans, A Geography of North American Indians.* Cherokee, NC: Cherokee Publications, 1977.

Pistorius, Anna. *What Indian Is It?* New York: Follett Publishing Company, 1956.

Reese, James V., and Lorrin Kennamer. *Texas Land of Contrast: Its History and Geography.* Austin, TX: W. S. Benson and Company, 1972.

Richardson, Rupert Norval. *Texas, The Lone Star State.* Englewood Cliffs, NJ: Prentice-Hall, Inc., 1981.

Rickard, J. A. *Brief Biographies of Brave Texans.* Dallas, TX: Banks Upshaw and Company, 1962.

Rollings, Willard H. *The Comanche.* New York: Chelsea House Publishers, 1989.

Sharpe, J. Ed. *The Cherokees, Past and Present.* Cherokee, NC: Cherokee Publications, 1970.

Shaw, Charles. *Indian Life in Texas.* Austin, TX: State House Press, 1987.

Shepherd, Sally. *Indians of the Plains.* Franklin Watts, Inc., 1976.

Steiner, Stan. *The Tiguas: The Lost Tribe of City Indians.* New York: Crowell-Collier Press, 1972.

Sullivan, Jerry M. "The Early Caddoes Texas' First Farmers." *Texas Parks and Wildlife,* January 1984, Vol. 42, 32–37.

Sutton, Feliz. *The How and Why Wonder Book of North American Indians.* Los Angeles: Price/Stern/Sloan, 1985.

Terrell, John Upton, *Apache Chronicle.* New York: World Publishing Times Mirror, 1972.

Waldman, Carl. *Encyclopedia of Native American Tribes.* New York: Facts on File Publications, 1988.

Warren, Betsy. *Let's Remember Texas Indians.* Dallas, TX: Hendrick-Long Publishing Company, 1981.

———. *Let's Look Inside a Tepee.* Austin, TX: RanchGate Books, 1989.

———. *Indians Who Lived in Texas.* Austin, TX: Steck-Vaughn Co., 1970.

Webb, Walter Prescott. *The Handbook of Texas.* Vol. 1, 592. Austin, TX: Texas State Historical Association, 1952

The New World Book. Vol. 17, 378–379. Chicago: Scott Fetzer Co., 1990.

The New World Book. Vol. 3, 325. Chicago: Scott Fetzer Co., 1990.

Wunder, John R. *The Kiowa.* New York: Chelsea House Publishers, 1989.

Audiovisual

The Alabama-Coushatta Indians. FS, The University of Texas Institute of Texan Cultures, San Antonio, TX.

The Land and the Early People. FS, Southwest Films Association, Brownwood, TX.

The Tigua Indians. FS, The University of Texas Institute of Texan Cultures, San Antonio, TX.

The Story of Texas (Indians of Texas). Video, Southwest Media Services, Dallas, TX, 1985.